English Life in the First World War

Overleaf. Patriotic London
crowds throw flowers to
wounded soldiers.

English Life in the First World War

Christopher Martin

"It seems as if we were all going to be dragged into the the danse macabre. One can only grin, and be fatalistic. My dear nation is bitten by the tarantula, and the venom has gone home at last. Now it is dance, *mes amis*, to the sound of the knuckle-bones."

D. H. Lawrence in a letter, 1916

WAYLAND PUBLISHERS LONDON

OTHER TITLES IN THE ENGLISH LIFE SERIES

Copyright © 1974 by Christopher Martin
First published 1974 by
Wayland (Publishers) Ltd
101 Gray's Inn Road London WC1
SBN 85340 417 8
Printed in Great Britain by Page Bros (Norwich) Ltd, Norwich

Contents

I 1914

"It will be the most popular war this country ever engaged in. Look out of the window now and you will see the people beginning to go mad."
J. Ramsay Macdonald, in a letter, August 1914.

The Outbreak of War

GREAT BRITAIN declared war on Germany at 11 p.m. on Tuesday, 4th August, 1914. The brilliant European summer of that year had been darkened by ever-growing crises since the assassination of the Archduke Franz-Ferdinand, heir to the throne of Austria-Hungary, at Serajevo in Bosnia on the 28th June. Austria declared war on Serbia, Russia's ally, accusing her of responsibility for the murder. The Russians backed Serbia; Germany supported the Austrians. A sad sequence of declarations of war followed. Diplomatic threats became real war as the huge conscript armies were mobilized. For Germany to attack Russia, she had also to attack France, Russia's ally, putting into operation the long considered Schlieffen plan, a huge wheeling army movement through Belgium to strike at Paris. Belgian neutrality was guaranteed by several powers including Britain, who was also France's ally. After the German assault on Belgium, starting on the 2nd August, a British ultimatum called upon Germany to withdraw. It expired at midnight on 4th August (at 11 p.m. British time).

There was no answer from Germany. *The Times* reporter, Michael Macdonagh, standing with London crowds in Parliament Square, watched Big Ben signal the coming of war: "The pause between each stroke and its reverberation seemed unusually prolonged . . . Was he booming out sweet peace and in red slaughter? At the eleventh stroke of the clock, the crowd . . . burst with one accord into 'God save the King.' There was no public proclamation that we were at war by a herald to the sound of trumpets and the beating of drums. The great crowd rapidly dispersed in all directions, most of them running to get home quickly, and as they ran they cried aloud rather hysterically, 'War! War! War!' "

Although war with Germany had been much discussed as a possibility during the first years of the century, the actual outbreak came almost by surprise. There had been tension between the great powers for many years. Britain and Germany had been trade and imperial rivals. Their particular arms race had been in battleships – the great heavily armoured Dreadnoughts – as each sought mastery of the world's seas. But, by 1914, the tension seemed to have subsided. Britain was preoccupied with her own internal problems, with severe industrial strife and a threatening civil war in Ireland over the intractable questions of Home Rule and Ulster. The European crisis only began to loom large in British thoughts at the end of July. A first reaction was to stand aside. A famous street

Opposite. Crowds at midnight on 4th August 1914 cheering King George V at Buckingham Palace on declaration of war.

7

Crowds in England (*left*) and Germany (*right*) on the declaration of war.

poster for the magazine *John Bull* declared, "To Hell with Serbia!" Gradually other ominous newspaper placards began to appear: "All Europe arming;" "The Brink of Catastrophe;" "Europe drifting to disaster;" "The horrid spectre of War." The Foreign Secretary, Edward Grey (1862–1933) spoke to the House of Commons on 28th June: "The world must prepare for the greatest catastrophe that has ever befallen the continent of Europe." Members of Parliament left the House "whispering gravely."

On Friday 31st July, the August Bank Holiday weekend, climax of the glorious summer, began. Already the feverish atmosphere had increased prices of food, and the rush to lay in stores of provisions started. The Bank Rate, the "thermometer" of crisis in the City of London, rose to 10 per cent. Over the weekend the British Fleet prepared to go to sea, anticipating the declaration. On the 3rd August, the British Regular Army was mobilized. Among the gaily dressed holiday-makers on busy stations moved khaki-clad soldiers and blue-jackets, with kit bags on their shoulders, saying goodbye to their families.

Hundreds of foreigners, notably Germans who had worked as waiters in hotels or as clerks in the City, were beginning a rush back to their own countries, some of them gathering to sing their own national anthems on the platforms. Bank Holiday Monday, with its radiant sunshine, became a dreamlike day of growing tension. In an era without radio, men eagerly purchased the latest edition of newspapers. Crowds in parks and on beaches discussed the news tremulously. In London, restless crowds moved from Whitehall to Buckingham Palace. Street traders selling Union Jacks did a roaring trade. "One could not stay in the house," wrote Mrs. C. S. Peel in her book, *How We Lived Then*. "There was a feeling as of an inner smouldering which at moments burst out into intense excitement. The red geraniums outside Buckingham Palace looked redder than they had ever looked before. The Palace, seen against the sky, appeared as if cut out of steel. It seemed as if inanimate things might suddenly become alive and do something . . . I prayed silently, 'O God, O God, don't let this war happen.'" Throughout the weekend, at nightfall, the crowd outside the Palace sang patriotic songs. There was the same mood in the provinces. At a Cambridge cinema, the latest war news, written on slides, was flashed up on the screen. The pianist, accompanying the silent film started to play "Rule Britannia" and the seven hundred strong audience joined in, and sang the whole verse and chorus, "finishing with a tremendous cheer." As a brilliant sun shone from a cloudless sky over that fateful weekend, excitement mounted. "Young men in straw hats . . . Girls in light callico dresses . . . all were already touched with war fever," wrote Macdonagh. "They saw England radiant through the centuries, valiant and invincible, and felt assured that so she will appear for, ever." So it was that the coming of war was celebrated in London with the same pathetic enthusiasm shown in other European capitals. Few realized what the new kind of war among advanced industrial nations would involve. Some of the nation's leaders could guess. Sir Edward Grey gloomily contemplated the White-hall crowds and said, "The lamps are going out all over Europe: we shall not see them lit again in our lifetime."

The First Effects of War

The immediate effects of the war were part of the general mood of hysteria. Panic food buying and hoarding continued. The 4th August was "a day of crisis in the shopping world." Grocers reported eight days' business done in one day, some shops selling out completely. People carried off car-loads of food, or brought dustbins and tubs to load with groceries. Angry poor women snatched parcels from the rich; shop delivery vans were held up and robbed. Prices, especially of petrol, rose rapidly. Arnold Bennett, the novelist, reported an Essex farmer "laying in ammunition against the time when the populace will raid the country-side demanding provisions." Gradually the official appeal to housewives to "act as you always act" calmed the panic. There was a similar rush for money as depositors withdrew their gold. The Bank Holiday was extended and the banks were closed until the end of the week, the great iron shutters drawn over the windows, making the City of London a strange place. The Stock Exchange ceased its dealings until it was allowed to re-open in January 1915. Gold sovereigns were called in and replaced by paper money, the first one pound and ten shilling notes.

War also disrupted the fragile, intricate business world at once, and caused immediate unemployment. Particularly hard hit were the clothing trade, especially the luxury sweatshops of the East End, the fishing industry, the hotel business and anyone involved in business with Germany. Charities, like the Prince of Wales's Relief Fund, or Queen Mary's Needlework Guild, set up in September, helped a little until the mushrooming new war industries brought not only work but compara-tive prosperity to the unemployed. The sudden departure of husbands and fathers to the Army, with the first confusion about the separation allowance for soldiers' wives (both this and the war widow's pension were pitifully small in 1914) made the first months difficult ones for the working class.

The most significant immediate change brought by war was the Defence of the Realm Act, passed rapidly by Parliament on 8th August. Barely noticed by the excited populace, D.O.R.A. virtually put Britain under Martial Law. After only five minutes' parliamentary discussion, long valued, hard won British personal liberties were signed away. Moreover D.O.R.A. was a "skeleton" Act, an approved general principle to which a multitude of amendments were added. People caught spying or communicating with the enemy, or found interfering with military installations could now be tried by court martial. Suspects could be arrested and imprisoned simply following an order from the Home Secretary. Later additions to the Act allowed the Government to take control of all energy supplies, or to seize any land they wanted, clear an area of its inhabitants, commandeer boats or vehicles, and arrest those causing "alarm or disaffection." D.O.R.A. was shown by cartoonists as a spinster aunt; in fact her powers were formidable. One contemporary said that it gave the State powers beyond that of the Stuart kings.

Departure of the B.E.F.

The British Expeditionary Force, the small but efficient Regular Army of seven divisions, with its tiny Royal Flying Corps, was at once sent to France to assist the French in holding the German invasion. The first days of war were full of emotion as soldiers said goodbye to their families. On stations throughout Britain, there were scenes of leave-taking. Bands played the soldiers off to battle. Typical were departures from Cambridge. A local journalist observed "the characteristic parting salute of one Englishman to another – a hard, slow grip of the hand and a hearty 'Goodbye old man, safe return' or 'So long, old chap, good luck' generally expressed sentiments too deep for words . . . The crowd sang 'Rule Britannia' in which the men joined heartily . . . wives and sweethearts came forward shyly for a parting kiss and a whispered 'God speed' . . The crowd raised a loud cheer and waved hats, handkerchiefs and Union Jacks. Just as the cheering subsided, the train began to move, and a childish voice piped 'Goodbye Daddy.'"

A troop train departs.

People living by the railways watched the trains pass. Mrs. Peel quotes two eye-witnesses. "I shall never forget the almost unending roar of troop-trains on the way to Southampton. My husband was one of the first to go, and through the long unhappy nights I lay listening to them." Another woman recalled, "I was coming home after a holiday . . . I waited, sitting on the platform, watching trains full of soldiers go past. Suddenly I felt the tears come . . . all these men . . . those boys . . . one could not bear it." The men of the B.E.F. were destined to take a gallant part in the first battles of the War, the Marne and first Ypres, where they were joined by Territorials from Britain's other part-time Army of volunteers. Their marching song, "It's a long, long way to Tipperary" became famous. So did the name they called themselves, the "Old Contemptibles" (the Kaiser was said to have called them "A contemptible little army").

A tender family farewell for a British sailor.

"Gallant little Belgium"

National leaders became busy justifying Britain's entry into war. The Prime Minister, Mr. Asquith (1852–1928) described Britain's motives in a speech to the House of Commons on 6th August. Britain was fighting "to fulfil a solemn international obligation . . . not only of law but of honour" and "to vindicate the principle that small nationalities are not to be crushed by the arbitrary will of a strong and over-mastering power." He summed up, "Britain had a duty to Belgium; she was bound by honour to support France." The ideas of Duty and Honour were echoed by a host of other authority figures. For example, Gilbert Murray, an Oxford don, wrote in a pamphlet, "Honour and dishonour are real things . . . Germany suddenly and without excuse invaded Belgium . . . our answer was: 'Evacuate Belgium within twelve hours or we fight you.' I think the answer was right . . . and I believe that the Government has rightly interpreted the feelings of the average British citizen." The Church quickly followed the State in accepting and applauding the war: it was justified as a spiritual struggle of good against evil. Everyone was relieved to see national purpose and unity again. David Lloyd George (1863–1945), then Chancellor of the Exchequer, spoke powerfully about the "purification" of British life: "the great flood of luxury and sloth which had submerged the land is receding, and a new Britain is appearing. We can see for the first time the fundamental things that matter in life and that have been obscured from our vision by the tropical growth of prosperity." The "feverish era of unbridled luxury" was over.

Gallant Little Belgium resists the German invader – a famous *Punch* cartoon.

The German treatment of Belgium was brutal enough to silence any remaining critics of the Government's action: the invaders pillaged conquered towns, shooting several thousand hostages as reprisals where civilians dared to fight back. The German policy, half accident, half calculated "frightfulness," was enough to unite British public opinion very quickly. John Galsworthy, the novelist, writing in the *Daily News* (which had been most outspoken against the declaration) was a typical convert: to him, Belgium was "this most gallant of little countries ground, be-

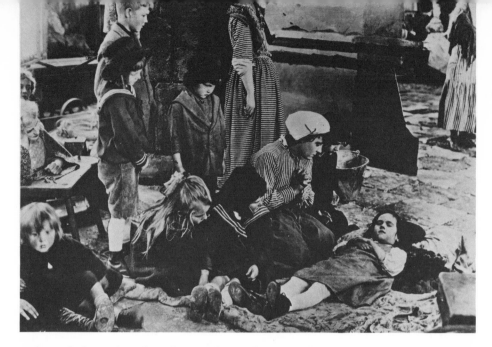

Comic ideas of the German spy, said to be lurking everywhere in Britain. Both drawn by Alfred Leete. *Below* "Schmidt the Spy." *Bottom.* Schmidt again. He reports "The English are living in fear of Zeppelin raids, and at night sentries in bomb-proof shelters are placed in the streets, armed with high-angle fire-guns and supplied with special telescopes."

cause of sheer loyalty, beneath an iron heel – this most innocent of sufferers from God's own Armageddon." The moving, if sentimental, spirit of martyred Belgium was represented in war pageants, like that watched by Macdonagh in London. A girl dressed in mourning walked barefoot. "She carried aloft the flag of her country, torn and tattered but still beautiful in its colours of black, yellow and red . . . On her delicately chiselled face there was an expression of pride and sorrow and devotion." Subsequent German harshness in Northern France, such as the burning of Louvain University Library or the shelling of Rheims Cathedral, were cleverly used by British propagandists to strengthen revulsion against German cruelty and to mock their lofty claims to a superior civilization, a "Kultur" of philosophers and poets.

Concern for "Gallant little Belgium" was forced to take a more practical form when thousands of Belgian refugees who had escaped across the North Sea as "boatloads of misery" in every kind of vessel, began arriving at East Coast ports. About 100,000 men, women and children crossed to Britain. The War Refugees Committee, formed on 24th August, received hundreds of generous offers of hospitality. The enthusiasm did not last. Later a small Belgian colony was set up in Durham (with its own Belgian beer and cakes), where refugees helped the war effort in making munitions.

Spymania and Rumour

In the absence of hard news "that jade rumour" flourished in Britain. A severe policy of censorship was followed by the Government's Press Bureau, set up in August. The state of national tension therefore produced wild stories, spread rapidly by word of mouth. Macdonagh described this first nervous mood of the British: "their nerves are still jangling and they are subject to hallucinations. They seem to be enveloped in a mysterious darkness, haunted by goblins." People believed what they expected. A great naval battle, the long awaited Trafalgar of Dreadnoughts, was said to have been fought in the North Sea in the first week of war. Spymania flourished. Leading suspects were the foreign governess "with something in her face" and a trunk "full of plans and

Belgian refugees. Many came
to England and their pathetic
plight did much to increase
the British people's support for
the war.

photographs," the foreign waiter with his dangerous-looking dining-
room table plan, the German barber planning to cut British throats, the
alien grocer selling poisoned food. Suburban householders with hard
tennis courts (easily converted into German gun-emplacements) were
also suspicious. Eastern England was especially full of spies, said
rumour. They were signalling to submarines, overpowering signalmen in
lonely railway signalboxes, driving about in "a dark closed car with a
green light on top," the four occupants in "strangely muffled head-gear."
Local papers record the exploits of intrepid boys tracking men seen
loitering on railway bridges. In Essex, Arnold Bennett described in his
diary the arrest of a local miller, "now proved to be a German officer
and plans of Harwich etc. have been found at his place."

Right. The Angels of Mons who were supposed to have assisted the B.E.F. in battle. This was the most fantastic, yet widely believed, war rumour.

Two strange stories show how credulous the population was in this first odd war atmosphere. In September, thousands of Russian troops were said to have passed through England on their way to help in France, train after long train running through with drawn blinds, only allowing glimpses of carriages packed with fierce-looking bearded men wearing fur hats. They had been seen on station platforms "stamping the snow from their boots" and "calling hoarsely for vodka." Railway porters at Edinburgh, it was said, had to sweep the snow from the carriages. The whole tale, it turned out, was fabricated, supposedly starting from a telegram to a grocer, promising "two hundred thousand Russian eggs are being despatched via Archangel." The legend of the Angels of Mons was a similar phenomenon. During the British Army's retreat from Mons in August, the writer, Arthur Machen, had composed a story, "The Bowmen" (published in the *Evening News*) in which he had imagined the hard-pressed British soldiers being helped by the ghosts of the victorious English bowmen of the medieval Battle of Crecy. Soon many variants of the tale were circulating, but claimed as literal truth. Wounded soldiers reported shining shapes, visions of St. George, angels, arrow wounds on enemy bodies. The Russian soldiers and the Angels, like most of the spies, were psychological phenomena, born of hysteria.

Invasion: Fears and Precautions

Fear of German invasion was very real in Britain and had been played on for years by popular journalists. In 1906 Lord Northcliffe's *Daily Mail* had run, as part of its campaign in support of compulsory military service, a serial by William Le Queux, called "The Invasion of 1910," in which the author anticipated a German landing on the East Coast and traced the subsequent conquest of Britain. A host of imitators copied the idea.

A lonely sentry guard against German invasion on an East Coast beach.

When war came, the stories of German atrocities in Belgium heightened the fears. Throughout the war a substantial force of soldiers and a heavy naval force were maintained to guard the East Coast. Defences were prepared: thus at Southwold in Suffolk, the Town Clerk reported the building of street barricades, a network of trenches and breast-works on the cliffs, and the placing of a boom across the harbour entrance. As late as 1918 plans were being discussed to build "pillbox" forts along the coast (near the remains of the Martello towers built to repel Napoleon). A severe blackout was imposed on East Coast towns.

Arrangements were made against German attack, published as a handbook for civilians: local gentry and clergy were to take charge; cattle and livestock were to be concealed; machinery was to be dismantled; motor vehicles and carts made useless; tools collected and hidden. Michael Macdonagh, after seeing a poster about invasion precautions, pondered, "What a catastrophe is here boded forth! Hordes of Germans landing on the South Coast and trampling through Sussex, Kent and Surrey on their way to London as they trampled across Belgium with rapine and slaughter in their wake!"

Although British sea power prevented any real invasion attempt, there were two kinds of German raid, which shocked the country. On 16th December, German cruisers daringly crossed the North Sea and shelled the East Coast resorts of Hartlepool, Whitby and Scarborough. 137 people were killed and 592 injured, and much damage was done. A girl cleaning her doorstep died at Scarborough; a family of eight perished at Hartlepool. It seemed extraordinary that ordinary civilians could die like this. Thousands flocked to see the damage, Sylvia Pankhurst among them: "The sky and sea were a leaden grey. The big amusement palaces on the front were scarred and battered by shell-fire, iron columns twisted and broken, brick work crumbling, windows gone.

German warships shell
Hartlepool in December 1914.

Yawning breaches disclosed the pictures and furnishings, riddled and rent by the firing, dimmed and discoloured by blustering winds and spray . . .'' The moral shock of this attack on civilians was enormous, and, incidentally, a great stimulus to recruiting.

The other raid was still more ill-omened. The first enemy aeroplane to appear over Britain attacked Dover on Christmas Eve 1914, dropping a single bomb. The greater threat came from the Zeppelin airships, which could carry substantial quantities of bombs. Although British people were still inclined to scoff at "the gasbags," the authorities made preparations against attack. On 11th September, the lights of London were dimmed as a move towards complete blackout. Macdonagh noted the changes: buses and trams curtained, car headlights turned off, street lamps dimmed with blue paint, house windows obscured by blinds. "So we have grown accustomed to look upwards in the dark. For the first time we have come to realize in London the beauty of the dark blue sky sparkling with the constellations." Sometimes the city skies were cut by protecting searchlights, "brilliant lines of light like gigantic flaming swords . . . What seek they? Zeppelins. They give us a sense of security against raiders who in the night time attempt to creep upon us and murder us, non-combatants, in our sleep."

Patriotism

Such threats from the enemy heightened the patriotic fervour produced by the first months of the war. "Men and women feel a love of country who never felt it before," wrote the journalist, G. S. Street. "Our fields and trees and inheritance and traditions and famous men – all are doubly dear now, and so are we to one another." Britain, with her ancient heritage of tradition and culture, seemed in danger. A mass of writing in patriotic vein celebrated love of country. The epic style was popular:

Left. A house wrecked after the German navy had shelled Scarborough, December 1914. This incident was used to stimulate more recruitment to the British army (*below*).

17

Patriotic postcard: the British lion ready for all enemies.

Searching the skies of London for Zeppelins. The blackout began in the autumn of 1914.

The oak of Empire; eagle, whose safe wings
Mother her brood of colonies; where rings
No chain of slave; O England, for the clang
And clash of battle, gird thy loins . . ."

The heroes of Britain's military past were recalled: Drake, Nelson, Grenville, Wellington. New heroes were invented. Lord Kitchener, the old hero of the Sudan wars, was the new British Lion. Sir John French, Commander of the B.E.F. and Admiral Jellicoe, the Naval leader, the King, George V, were other idols. Their faces appeared on postcards, on badges, on cinema screens. The singing of the National Anthem enjoyed a new vogue in theatres and cinemas. "Rule Britannia," "Land of Hope and Glory" and "Tipperary" also reflected the patriotic cult of 1914.

Kitchener's Armies

Patriotic young men found a practical outlet for their enthusiasm to serve "The Cause," when Lord Kitchener (1850–1916), Secretary of State for War, announced an appeal for volunteers for his projected New Armies. Kitchener was shrewd in foreseeing a long war of several years.

Below left. England, Scotland and Ireland temporarily united against the Germans. A postcard.

Below. The national hero Lord Kitchener, Secretary of State for War, shown on a postcard.

"AND BRITONS ALL CAN AND WILL DIE TO A MAN, ERE THEY GIVE UP A GRAIN OF THE ISLAND."
Old Song by T. Dibdin.

Field-Marshal Earl Kitchener.

Hats off to the Flag
we all love and adore,
And give it a mighty
great cheer,
For with gallant Commanders
like this to the fore—
Old England has
nothing to fear.

British naval power would not be enough. "The British Empire must bear its part on a scale proportionate to its magnitude and power," Kitchener told the Cabinet. "We must be prepared to put armies of millions in the field . . ." His first appeal was published on 6th August:

YOUR KING AND COUNTRY NEED YOU.
A CALL TO ARMS.

An addition of 100,000 men to his Majesty's Regular Army is immediately necessary in the present grave National Emergency. Lord Kitchener is confident that this appeal will be at once responded to by all who have the safety of our Empire at heart . . .

GOD SAVE THE KING.

A Parliamentary Recruiting Committee was formed, that began a poster campaign to draw recruits for Kitchener's "gigantic experiment." Fifty-four million posters were issued. Their message rang from all sides. Michael Macdonagh described the scene in London: "The town is vibrant with the call to arms. Posters appealing for recruits are to be seen on every hoarding, in most shop windows, on omnibuses, tram cars and commercial vehicles. The great base of the Nelson pillar is covered with them . . . Everywhere, Lord Kitchener points a monstrously big finger, exclaiming, 'I want you!' Another bill says: 'Lord Kitchener wants 100,000 men!', 'Rally round the flag,' 'Every fit man wanted,' 'Forward to Victory,' 'Enlist Now!'" Alfred Leete's famous drawing of the pointing Kitchener was much the best of the first wave of Union Jack and John Bull patriotism. Later, more cunning poster appeals were made to a man's shame. One ran:

"There are three types of men:
Those who hear the call and obey.
Those who delay.
And the others.
To which do you belong?"

More subtle were those aimed at women, who were to persuade their menfolk to join the Forces. One poster was addressed "To the young women of London."
"Is your best boy wearing khaki? If not, don't you think he should be?"
"If he does not think that you and your country are worth fighting for – do you think he is worthy of you?"
"Don't pity the girl who is alone: her young man is probably a soldier, fighting for her and his country and for you."
Recruiting "poets" added their voice. The following appeared in *The Times* in August:

"As though Youth had not all the best, this day
Offers him one excelling best-of-all –
The glorious summons of a trumpet-call
To prove his manhood in man's noblest fray
To be with those who fight at last to slay
That ancient despot, war . . ."

A flood of men came forward, 30,000 a day by the end of the first

YOUR COUNTRY'S CALL

Isn't this worth fighting for?
ENLIST NOW

Daddy, what did YOU do in the Great War?

month. Over two million had volunteered for the five New Armies by the time conscription was introduced in early 1916.

Great queues formed outside recruiting offices; men walked miles to join. There were men from all walks of life. It was, commentators noted with some relief, remembering the class conflict of the previous decade, a "new democracy." Motives for joining were as varied as the men: some sought adventure and glamour; some wanted escape from routine; some were angry about Belgium; many came from industrial or mining areas, attracted by an open air life. Patriotic enthusiasm and genuine idealism were the basis for recruitment in Kitchener's Armies. All the more bitter was the waste of so many Kitchener men in the futilities of Loos, Gallipoli and the Somme, where generals were "content to fight machine-gun bullets with the breasts of brave men."

Some Kitchener battalions were raised by prominent people or by business organizations. At one end of the social scale were the Sportsmen's Battalions of "upper and middle class men, physically fit, able to shoot and ride," or the Public Schools Battalions. Such units absorbed the "nut," the pre-war, upper class dandy. Harold Owen described him as "an elegant idler, strenuous only in getting 'the last ounce' out of his motor-car. . . . He cultivated a manner almost effeminate. . . Golf was too strenuous for him and most things 'too much fag!' . . . Then with the

Recruiting posters for the New Armies, that on the left relying on simple patriotism, the one on the right appealing to guilt and shame.

Above. Keen volunteers queue outside a recruiting office to answer Kitchener's call to arms.

war the 'nut' vanished and the Young Briton leapt to life. The call of his race was answered in his blood and his fripperies dropped from him. . . The despair of many a father's heart became one of the glories of his race. . . He now lies under many a white cross in the fair land of France. . .''

From less wealthy parts of society came the Pals' Battalions formed in many Northern and Midland Industrial towns from men of similar occupation who all volunteered together. The idea began in Liverpool with the "Commercials" from various Liverpool trades. A Liverpool reporter watched the first "Pals" march through the city: "There was no vain glory about this display – there was just the tramp, tramp of smart, well set-up young gentlemen, shoulders thrown back and faces stern and resolute, denoting a determination to go forward with a duty in the cause of civilization." Tragically, many of the "Pals," with their wonderful sense of comradeship, were to die together in the bloody Somme massacre on 1st July, 1916.

There was a desperate shortage of equipment. The men did not mind drilling with broomsticks or learning to shoot with dummy artillery, but they did regret the lack of uniforms. One of their songs ran:

"Where are our uniforms?
Far, far away.
When will our rifles come?
P'raps, p'raps some day."

22

The volunteers drilled in parks, squares, school-yards or on beaches in their civilian clothes. Lucky ones received fragments of uniforms. Others got temporary blue serge suits. Macdonagh watched a parade at Aldershot in September and commented on the motley dress: "Some were only half made up, wearing scarlet jacket, the kilt, or trews of the old Army uniform, mingled with articles of civilian attire, all in glaring contrast. . . There was . . . a diversified and discordant display of straw hats, bowlers and tweed caps. What particularly interested me was the sight of many wearers of tall hats, frock coats and spatted boots – lion hearts beating under the height of fashion. Others had the appearance of tramps." By early 1915, the new factories had managed to supply the keenly awaited, proudly worn khaki. Men spent happy days training in England marching and digging, enjoying the open air and comradeship, the feeling of purpose, the ritual of army life. Everywhere were new encampments, the sound of bugle calls, lines of marching men. By Christmas in London *The Times* reporter observed, "There is khaki everywhere. Long lines of whistling, singing khaki tramp down Oxford Street or Piccadilly. The parks are full of drilling khaki."

People everywhere had family links with the New Armies and there was widespread pride in "The Soldier Son." The late Victorian contempt for "Tommy Atkins," was forgotten. There was no real need for the "Hats off to Recruits League," formed to improve the soldier's image.

The civilian population had little desire to consider the sorry long or short term effects of rushing a whole generation of men into khaki. The men themselves were keen to test themselves. F. H. Keeling, a volunteer sergeant, wrote home "Assuming this war had to come, I feel nothing but gratitude to the gods for sending it in my time." Many Kitchener volunteers were fated for death or mutilation in battle. Watching them train on the beach, Edward Thomas (who was to die in battle himself) seemed to anticipate their fate: "The recruits are drilling on the shore

New Army men, in uniform at last, parade the streets.

in mist, opening and closing in ghostly silence. For their feet make no sound on the sand, and the calm sea, sucking at the rocks, drowns the shout of the sergeant and all other noise but a dog barking at the waves. The boys watch in silence."

The First Christmas

Christmas came with few signs as yet of wartime austerity: shops were packed with goods; food was plentiful, especially luxuries, which had fallen in price due to the decline in entertaining; war toys were popular. This was the landmark looked forward to in August, when everyone had said, "It will be over by Christmas." Instead the war was only just beginning. After the First Battle of Ypres in October, the Western Front froze into the position, beginning the horrors of trench warfare. Barbed wire and machine gun, triumphant in defence, prevented the front from moving again until 1918. The trench soldiers celebrated the season with a bizarre Christmas truce, meeting the Germans in No-man's land between the lines to exchange gifts. The original B.E.F. was by now almost destroyed. The wounded, in their strange bright blue, red and white uniforms, were already becoming familiar in British towns. Huge banners, saying "Quiet for the wounded" hung over straw-covered streets outside London Hospitals. As the bells rang to celebrate (they were later silenced under D.O.R.A.) many homes were already mourning the death of a loved one. A poem by Austin Dobson, in the Christmas issue of the magazine *Sphere* summed up:

> "What do you clear bells ring to me
> In this glad hour of jubilee?
> Not joy, not joy. I hear instead:
>   So many dead! So many dead!"

A Kitchener volunteer leaves his proud family to serve his country.

2 *1915*

"And the war news always coming, the war horror
drifting in, drifting in, prices rising, excitement growing,
people going mad about the Zeppelin raids. And
always the one song:
'Keep the home fires burning,
Though your hearts be yearning . . .'"

D. H. Lawrence, *Kangaroo*.

Zeppelin Raids

THE GERMAN ZEPPELINS were huge, dirigible airships, some 650 feet long, their great hulls containing the two million cubic feet of hydrogen that lifted them into the air. They had been used as passenger carriers before the war and had become flying symbols of German prestige. In war, they were employed by the Navy and the Army as bombers, carrying a weapon load of 27 tons. They were dangerous to fly, and the brave crews wore padded boots to avoid the fatal spark that might set off the gas, petrol and explosive that surrounded them. They were vulnerable, too, in strong winds, slow and clumsy, steered only by primitive compass. Yet the "long, sinuous airship" became a very real terror to Britain in 1915.

The German Zeppelin commanders pressed the Kaiser, William II, for permission to attack. In early 1915 he reluctantly agreed to allow bombing of military targets, exempting residential districts of London and historic buildings, especially the Royal Palaces. In January 1915, the first raiders visited East Anglia: Great Yarmouth received the first bombs; King's Lynn also suffered. Four people were killed. Astonished onlookers heard the engines as "an ominous grinding . . . growing in volume – throbbing, pulsating . . . filling the air with its sound. Then huge reports smote the ear, shattering, deafening. . ." As bombs fell, "great flashes of light leaped up." Little was seen of the airships themselves except "two bright stars moving apparently thirty yards apart." One man saw the ship "the biggest sausage I ever saw in my life . . . like a church steeple sideways."

During the dark, moonless nights of the spring, other attacks followed, mostly on East Anglian towns. The German airmen were condemned in the Press as "baby killers" or "apostles of Hun frightfulness." The defences were totally inadequate. Frustration was relieved by spymania against the "brilliantly lighted motor-car with two powerful head-lights" that was said to be guiding the enemy.

In autumn came the first attacks on London itself. In September, the Zeppelins struck at the Commercial City, what German newspaper propaganda colourfully called "the heart which pumps the life blood into the arteries of the brutal huckster nation." The ship dropped its bombs between Euston and Tower Bridge, narrowly missing the Bank of England, and causing huge fires in the soft goods warehouses by the river. The raid caused half a million pounds worth of damage and killed thirty-eight people. The shock of the attack was far greater than the

Opposite. The Zeppelin: a 1915 cartoon from the *Graphic* captioned "Gas-bag or Terror – Which?" No-one knew exactly what the Kaiser's new weapon could do.

Below. Zeppelins over Southend, May 1915. Astonished citizens leave their beds to watch the strange new enemy.

A German drawing showing a Zeppelin over the Tower of London and Tower Bridge. The first Zeppelin attack on London came in September 1915.

Opposite. With the threat of air-raids, an official poster taught the public to distinguish hostile and friendly aircraft.

physical damage. There was the strangeness of the experience for eye-witnesses: one, reported by Mrs. Peel, remembered "an odd chunkety, chunkety noise. It sounded as if a tram with rusty wheels were travelling through the sky." Macdonagh saw the ship, "a long narrow object of a silvery hue. I felt like what a watcher of the skies must feel like when a new planet swims into his ken." Another eye-witness wrote, "As seen from below, the airship gave an impression of absolute calm and absence of hurry." In fact, brisk artillery fire had made the airship turn from its last target, Tower Bridge, to drop its last bombs on Liverpool Street Station. Here a London bus was blown to pieces, while passengers waited uneasily in blacked-out trains, as bombs crashed nearby.

The first effect of this raid was curiosity as thousands of Londoners rushed outside to see the Zeppelin, a novel "entertainment." The rain of shrapnel on the roofs and the bombs themselves sent them hurrying for shelter. Next day crowds gathered to see the damage, and real fear began. That first concern voiced when Bleriot flew the Channel in 1909 was now realized. As Macdonagh expressed it: "England's insularity was at an end. . . Her Navy could no longer keep her safe from enemy entry into her island fortress. It was the end of an old song."

When the Zeppelins returned in October, fear had turned to panic. At the warning cry of "Zepps! Zepps," men ran through the streets,

28

PUBLIC WARNING

The public are advised to familiarise themselves with the appearance of British and German Airships and Aeroplanes, so that they may not be alarmed by British aircraft, and may take shelter if German aircraft appear. **Should hostile aircraft be seen,** take shelter **immediately** in the nearest available house, preferably in the basement, and remain there until the aircraft have left the vicinity : do not stand about in crowds **and do not touch unexploded bombs.**

In the event of **HOSTILE** aircraft being seen in country districts, the nearest Naval, Military or Police Authorities should, if possible, be advised immediately by Telephone of the TIME OF APPEARANCE, the DIRECTION OF FLIGHT, **and whether the aircraft is an Airship or an Aeroplane.**

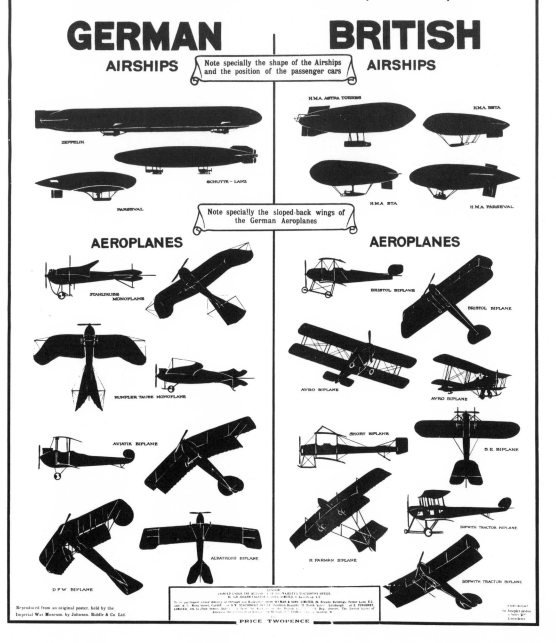

GERMAN | ## BRITISH

AIRSHIPS

Note specially the shape of the Airships and the position of the passenger cars

AIRSHIPS

ZEPPELIN

SCHUTTE – LANZ

PARSEVAL

H.M.A. ASTRA TORRES

H.M.A. BETA

H.M.A. ETA

H.M.A. PARSEVAL

Note specially the sloped-back wings of the German Aeroplanes

AEROPLANES

STAHLTAUBE MONOPLANE

RUMPLER TAUBE MONOPLANE

AVIATIK BIPLANE

ALBATROSS BIPLANE

D.F.W. BIPLANE

AEROPLANES

BRISTOL BIPLANE

BRISTOL BIPLANE

AVRO BIPLANE

AVRO BIPLANE

SHORT BIPLANE

B.E. BIPLANE

SOPWITH TRACTOR BIPLANE

H. FARMAN BIPLANE

SOPWITH TRACTOR BIPLANE

LONDON
PRINTED UNDER THE AUTHORITY OF HIS MAJESTY'S STATIONERY OFFICE.
By Sir JOSEPH CAUSTON & SONS, LIMITED, 9, Eastcheap, E.C.
To be purchased, either directly or through any Bookseller, from WYMAN & SONS, LIMITED, 29, Breams Buildings, Fetter Lane, E.C. and 54, St. Mary Street, Cardiff ; or H.M. STATIONERY OFFICE (Scottish Branch), 23, Forth Street, Edinburgh ; or E. PONSONBY, LIMITED, 116, Grafton Street, Dublin ; or from the Agencies in the British Colonies and Dependencies, The United States of America, the Continent of Europe and Abroad of T. FISHER UNWIN, London, W.C.

PRICE TWOPENCE

The Zeppelins seemed another example of German "frightfulness." A British soldier vows vengeance.

banging at the doors of houses where even the slightest glimmer of light showed, and a lighted cigarette or struck match was enough to earn a man a blow. An American journalist, W. G. Shepherd, described the Zeppelin's arrival: "Traffic is at a standstill. A million quiet cries make a subdued roar. Seven million people of the biggest city in the world stand gazing into the sky from the darkened streets. Here is the climax of the twentieth century. Among the autumn stars floats a long, gaunt Zeppelin. It is a dull yellow, the colour of the harvest moon. The long fingers of searchlights, reaching up from the roofs of the city, are touching all sides of the death messenger with their white tips. . ."

This Zeppelin crossed the Houses of Parliament, to the astonishment of M.P.s, and dropped bombs on London's theatre land. Twenty people were killed outside the Lyceum Theatre. Inside, a startled audience listened to the crashes, and a young officer on leave was heard to cry, "It's no business to happen here." The glare from burning buildings, the smell of escaping gas, the shattered water-mains, the grotesque casualties reminded onlookers of pictures of the San Francisco earthquake. The airships provoked a brave response from *The Times*: "Their effect is, not a demand for peace, but a demand of the whole nation to help in the war." The cry for reprisals began to be heard, but in vain, as Britain had no large airships.

Propaganda and Hatred

The mounting casualties, the air-raids, the rumours of German atrocities, cleverly played upon by official propagandists, created a dark, neurotic atmosphere of hate in Britain during 1915.

Smouldering resentment against Germans burst out in ferocious hatred after the sinking of the Cunard Liner *Lusitania* by a German submarine on 7th May. Over a thousand people were drowned, and their corpses were photographed on Irish beaches to stimulate British war hatred. The dead children seemed particularly poignant. In a newspaper cartoon they were pictured appealing, "But why did you kill us?" Rioting crowds furiously attacked German owned shops in the East End of London and other cities. The windows of those with foreign sounding names were smashed and their goods looted. The shopkeepers were savaged by the mob. Sylvia Pankhurst saw such an incident: "A woman was in the midst of a struggling mob, her blouse half torn off, her fair hair fallen, her face contorted with pain and terror, blood running down her bare white arm. A big drunken man flung her to the ground. She was lost to sight. . . 'Oh My God! Oh! They are kicking her!' a woman screamed. . . Alas, poor patriotism, what foolish cruelties are committed in thy name!" From the City of London, Members of the Stock Exchange, dressed in top hats and business suits, marched on the Houses of Parliament, demanding that the 24,000 Germans in Britain should be interned. They had already excluded German members from their Exchange, and two large German banks had been seized. In the Commons, Members of Parliament were "foaming at the mouth" against aliens.

This kind of pressure forced Prime Minister Asquith to take action: enemy aliens from seventeen to forty-five were to be interned. Old men,

The sinking of the liner *Lusitania* by a German submarine, May 1915, as depicted in the *Illustrated London News*.

Angry London crowds attack
and loot a German-owned shop
in the East End.

German prisoners and "aliens"
are marched to internment.

women and children were to be repatriated. The internees were concentrated on the Isle of Man, though thousands of London's former waiters, cooks, barbers, tailors and German clerks were to be found at Alexandra Palace, where they lived in modest comfort through the war.

Internment was but one result of the long campaign of hate run by the Press since the beginning of the war. The extremist editor of *John Bull*, Horatio Bottomley (1860–1933), advised, "If by chance you should discover one day in a restaurant that you are being served by a German waiter, you will throw the soup in his foul face; if you find yourself sitting at the side of a German clerk, you will spill the inkpot over his vile head."

The cry soon went up against the "pro-Germans" in Government. Prince Louis of Battenburg, First Sea Lord at the Admiralty, a naturalized Briton related to the Royal Family, was dismissed after a "whispering campaign" against him during 1914, despite his valuable work in preparing the British fleet for war. In 1915, the Lord Chancellor, Haldane (1856–1928), whose work had created the efficient British Expeditionary Force and the Territorial Army, was also dismissed. He was considered "a German in disguise", having once declared, in his love of German art and thought, that Germany was his "spiritual home." At the same time, the King removed the German Kaiser and the Emperor of Austria from the roll of Knights of the Garter, and the high honorary ranks they held in the British armed forces. People with German names were well advised to change them: Bernstein to Curzon, Steineke to Stanley, Stohwasser to Stowe, Rosenhein to Rose and so on. The King himself was to change his own family name from Saxe-Coburg-Gotha to Windsor in 1917.

The flames of hate were kept burning by official propaganda, prepared at the ever-growing Government Department at Wellington House, run increasingly by successful newspaper men. Shortly after the sinking of the *Lusitania*, the Bryce Report was published, with lucky timing, inquiring into the conduct of German Armies in Belgium during the first months of the war. Strangely morbid rumours of alleged cruelties had already been circulated. Here they were presented as "truth" in an official document (which was aimed particularly to win neutral America to the allied cause). Hundreds of "eye-witnesses" reported the sadistic cruelties they supposedly saw. One recalled a child murder by a soldier who "drove his bayonet into the child's stomach, lifting the child into the air on his bayonet, and carrying it away, he and his comrades still singing." There was the celebrated child with amputated hands: "We saw a boy of about twelve with a bandage where his hand should be . . . we were told the Germans had cut off his hand because he clung to his parents who were being thrown on the fire." The Report made excellent propaganda, with its vivid detail and sadistic appeal. However, most of it was probably lies. Propaganda made much of the other German barbarities, real or fancied: the execution of Nurse Edith Cavell in Belgium as a "spy;" the crucified Canadian found nailed to a door; the later tale of the German "corpse factory" where bodies from the battle-field were said to be melted down into useful fats. (This calculated lie was manufactured by reversing the captions on pictures

Propaganda poster warning people not to trust the Germans in future.

The image of the "Hun" and his atrocities in Belgium. From *Punch*.

Opposite. Drunken Germans looting in Belgium. A typical 1915 propaganda drawing. Published in the *Illustrated London News*.

"Give him his due." The Kaiser rewards one of his Devils. A Will Dyson cartoon.

of dead horses and dead men.) British official propaganda was dishonest, but, in its time, effective.

The press coarsely echoed the themes and tone of the official hate. The papers were free only to express opinions, which often seem hysterical, even insane. Germans to them were "malign spirits, steeped in depravity and lewdness." This is the *Daily Graphic*'s comment on the enemy: "Your German is a born bully, saturated with arrogance. His mind is diseased." After the sinking of the *Lusitania*, the same paper's voice became more bitter and shrill with hate: "Germany has run amok. . . The sportsman is not generous to vermin, and we have now reached a point when it becomes clear to everybody that the moral conscience of the German people is no higher than that of wolves or rats . . . the only safe course is to treat all persons of German birth as tainted with the virus which has converted the German nation into a gigantic plague spot. The brand of dishonour has been stamped upon the whole race. . . It must be treated by us as a war to the death."

All the vices of the enemy seemed concentrated in the much caricatured figures of Kaiser William II (1859–1940) and his son, the Crown Prince, "Little Willie." The Kaiser was "The mad dog of Europe," "The Beast of the Apocalypse," "A scourge the like of which the world has never seen before." A *Daily Mail* writer said of him, "The madman is piling up the logs of his own pyre. We can have no terror of the monster; we shall clench our teeth in determination that, if we die to the last man, the modern Judas and his Hell-begotten brood shall be wiped out. . . Our great England will shed its blood willingly to rid civilization of a criminal monarch and a criminal court which have succeeded in creating, out of a docile people, a herd of savages." William was shown as both satanic and ludicrous; it was almost forgotten that he was the son of one of Queen Victoria's daughters.

The best known of the unofficial propagandists was Horatio Bottomley, whose popular magazine, *John Bull*, made him a household name. His paper attacked firms with German trade links, and advertisements began to proclaim nervously "exclusively the product of British capital, British labour and British material." The pages of *John Bull*, like Bottomley's rousing sentimental speeches, have an undeniable power, especially when they attack "Germhuny," "The Frankenstein of iniquity," "the hideous monster whose fangs drip with the blood of millions." Bottomley preached total war: "I hold that we are justified in any measures . . . that will shorten by one day . . . the life of this man-eating monster, the Butcher of Berlin. . . He is the Hun – cruel, pitiless, ruthless, murderous. . ." Bottomley was the worst sort of war profiteer, winning himself some £27,000 for his jingoistic speeches, and thousands more from the sale of fraudulent "war bonds," a crime for which he was imprisoned after the war.

Military Mania

In the first year of the war, public attention focussed on the "khaki hero," the soldier in uniform seen in every town. The bronze-faced soldier on leave walked the London parks with "his attendant group

Britain infected by war fever: Mark Gertler's painting *The Merry-Go Round*.

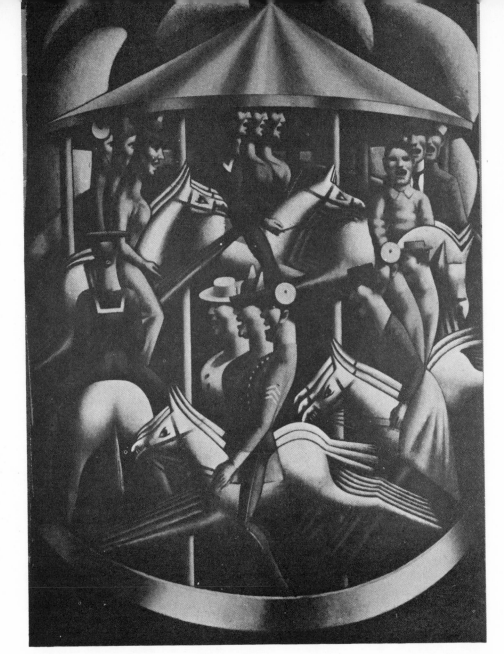

of girl worshippers." The wounded were especially popular, and were often invited to stay at large country houses, or were driven about London or taken to theatres by upper class hosts. Town halls, schools, town houses of wealthy people were converted into temporary hospitals for them.

In windows of houses everywhere, even the humblest country cottages, cards were displayed announcing proudly, "A man from this house is serving in the forces."

Memorials connected with previous conflicts excited a new public interest. In Hyde Park, Macdonagh noticed that even the familiar Achilles Statue, set up by English women to commemorate the achievements of Wellington, was looked up to with admiring eyes and its inscription eagerly read over. The Crimean monuments were also popular again, especially those dedicated to the Guards and to Florence Nightingale.

On suburban stations Macdonagh saw proud fathers handing round their sons' letters, "unstamped envelopes with strange postmarks and

uncouth cancellations . . . short and roughly scrawled, dated only 'from the Front,' 'At Sea' or 'In Base Hospital on Active Service.'" Sometimes these letters were printed in local newspapers. Here are some extracts from the Leicester press, typical fragments of war by anecdote, making the fighting seem glorious. "Our captain was laid low, mortally wounded. He lay in the trench and just before he died we captured our last objective and he went west, saying 'Bravo, England'. . ." Another man wrote, "War is a fine thing for a young man and I am glad I am able to take part in this one. Of course you have to chance your life but if I have to go west, mother, I'll go with a big heart. . ."

If khaki was the popular colour of the hour (women even had khaki dresses and "a veil with a tiny aeroplane upon it" was considered chic), the black of mourning was increasingly seen in the streets. Women and children went about in black clothes; dyers were kept busy altering coloured garments. Social prestige demanded full mourning in the first part of the war, although there were suggestions in the Press that a purple, or white, armlet would suffice to "express the pride we feel

Above left. **The Khaki hero and his girl: a sentimental postcard.**

Above right. **A letter from the trenches: a soldier's parents proudly read their son's news.**

in knowing that those who are nearest and dearest have given their lives in their country's cause." It was still possible to romanticize the soldier's death. At Easter, 1915, Dean Inge, of St. Paul's Cathedral, addressed "thousands of English parents, and young widows, and young orphans, who on this Easter day were thinking of the hastily made graves in a foreign land, where their dearest are sleeping." As consolation, continued this *Times* report, he read them a sonnet, recently composed by the young soldier poet, Rupert Brooke (soon to die himself on his way to the ill fated Gallipoli offensive in Turkey). It began:

> "If I should die, think only this of me:
>   That there's some corner of a foreign field
> That is for ever England. There shall be
>   In that rich earth a richer dust concealed;
> A dust whom England bore, shaped, made aware,
>   Gave, once, her flowers to love, her ways to roam,
> A body of England's, breathing English air,
>   Washed by the rivers, blest by suns of home . . .

"Pure and elevated patriotism . . . had never found a nobler expression," commented Dean Inge. Brooke's poem, and "Into Battle" by his friend, Julian Grenfell, seemed to sum up the gallant selfless idealism of the first months of the war, and to provide consolation for those whose relatives had fallen. Their poems were imitated in the vogue for "soldier-poets" that swept the country in 1915. "The whole nation has become a nest of singing birds," wrote one critic while another, Douglas Gold-

Sentimental patriotism: "The Tale of a Glorious End," published in the *Illustrated London News*. A fellow officer tells how the family's only son was killed.

38

ring, described in his book, *Reputations*, how, "lying about in every smart London drawing room you would find the latest little volume, and at every fashionable bookshop the half-crown war poets were among the best selling lines. We were asked to believe that the European war . . . had really brought to light a wealth of poetic talent." Most of this poetry was crude and sentimental, if well meaning. Here is a piece by "Rifleman Cox," which copies from Rupert Brooke rather obviously.

> "If I should fall, grieve not that one so weak
>   And poor as I
>   Should die
> Nay, though thy heart should break
> Think only this: That when at dusk they speak
> Of sons and brothers of another one
> Then thou canst say 'I too, had a son;
> He died for England's sake . . .!' "

There were best sellers in prose, too, like Ian Hay's *The First Hundred Thousand*, describing life in Kitchener's Army. There was an appetite for books about Allied war aims, or for those with titles like *The Soul of Germany*, describing enemy defects.

The war was also glamorized in pictures. In the absence, initially, of photography and films at the Front, impressions of battle were drawn by artist illustrators, working for weekly magazines. They showed war as a chivalrous game, packed with "Thin Red Line" or "Charge of the Light Brigade" incidents. Sentimental pictures were sold as prints in

The Shirker who has not volunteered for the Army (*left*), and the man who has joined up. Cartoon by Frank Reynolds in the *Illustrated London News*.

The Charge:
"Straight at the Guns the Lancers Rode," published in the *Illustrated London News*. This was war as people on the Home Front liked to see it.

their thousands: the dying horse in the famous "Goodbye, Old Pal," the wounded soldier's last message to his mother. This was the war as the Home Front wanted to see it, not its reality: the squalid misery of trenches, the bungled action of the 1915 battles, Neuve Chapelle and Loos, or Gallipoli.

Slackers and Derby Men

While casualties mounted, pressure increased on "slackers," who were not joining the Army. The sacrifices of war seemed unevenly divided. A letter in *The Times* in August 1914, had shown the way to treat "shirkers:" "Yesterday afternoon – every lawn tennis court in the space near me was crowded by strapping young Englishmen and girls. Is there no way of shaming these laggards? The English girl who will not know the man – lover, brother, friend – that cannot show an overwhelming reason for not taking up arms – that girl will do her duty and will give good help to her country." An advertisement in the same paper followed this idea: "Jack F.G. – If you are not in khaki by the 20th I shall cut you dead – Ethel M." Young women began giving out white feathers, the badge of cowardice, to men still in civilian dress. Macdonagh watched this happen on a London tram: two young men were set upon by three girls: "One of the girls was a pretty wench. She dishonoured one of the young men . . . by sticking a white feather in his button hole, and a look of contempt spoiled for a moment her lovely face." The novelist, Baroness Orczy, formed an Active Service League. In a letter to the *Daily Mail*, she defined its purpose: "Influencing sweethearts, brothers, sons and friends to recruit. Pledge: I hereby pledge myself most solemnly in the name of my King and Country, to persuade every man I know to offer his services to his country and I also pledge myself never to be seen in public with any man, who, being in every way free and fit, has refused to respond to his country's call." Badges were issued to the twenty-thousand women who joined the League.

"Slackers" attending football matches (which, like racing, went on as usual until 1917) were accused by posters carried by sandwich men: "Are you forgetting that there's a war on? Your country needs you. Be ready to defend your home and women from the German Huns!" Even in the music hall, there were accusing songs, like that of the famous star, Phyllis Dare:

> "Oh, we don't want to lose you
> But we think you ought to go . . . ."

Under the motto, "Wake up, London!" columns of soldiers marched through London to attract recruits. Sergeants wearing red, white and blue rosettes approached likely looking young men in the watching crowds. There were continual rallies in Trafalgar Square.

Workers on large estates, or servants in big houses were sometimes taken to enlist en masse by their employers: footmen, butlers, game-keepers, gardeners, coachmen, motor car drivers became "volunteers" together. Thus it came about that tents and wooden huts sprang up

Left and below. Recruiting in London.

like magic in country districts, and "the voice of the drill sergeant is heard in the land."

The casualties of the 1915 battles made it clear, however, that volunteers alone would not fill all the Army's needs. The voluntary system also took men unwisely from vital war industries. During 1915 the Government began to move towards conscription. The first stage was the National Register of July. To get a clearer picture of the nation's manpower, everyone between fifteen and sixty-five was to be noted on a register. Their willingness to undertake war work was also recorded. Thereafter all carried registration cards.

The next stage came in October with the appointment of the popular Lord Derby (1865–1948), "a strongly built, red-faced John Bull Englishman," as Director of Recruitment. His Derby scheme that ran in the last months of 1915 was a final chance for the voluntary system. All men between eighteen and forty-one (their names had already been recorded in the National Register) were asked to "attest" – to say

Special Constables, distinguished by striped armbands.

A women's sewing party making clothes for soldiers.

they would join the Army when called. The King added his special plea to "men of all classes to come forward voluntarily and take your share in the fighting." Single men would be called first. Men in "reserved" occupations, like munition-making or coalmining, were exempted. Despite a large-scale propaganda campaign, and the issue of arm-bands to attested men to save them from white feather humiliation, the scheme was a failure. Public opinion, still convinced of the existence of thousands of "slackers," was now prepared to accept conscription.

"Doing your bit"

The two catchphrases of 1915, "Doing your bit" and "Carry on," summed up the attitude of most civilians. An anonymous pamphlet "Carry on: Your duty in wartime," offered advice to the Home Front on how to behave in wartime: "There must be pluck in the office, and the shop and the factory, and in the house. . . The ships that sweep the seas, the khaki cohorts that march in glory, the unnamed heroes, trampled dead to make a bridge to victory, may thrill you with pride in the majesty of human power. But you, too, may be . . . a combatant in the great cause, comporting yourself as a hero or a craven . . . your part is to live plainly, pay promptly, apply your mental and physical powers to the benefit of the commonwealth. . ."

Men too old to be soldiers could serve as "special constables," replacing policemen who had gone into the army. 20,000 men showed their patriotism by signing on within twenty days of the outbreak of war. At first distinguished only by a striped armband, the "special" eventually went on patrol in a smart black uniform. After his day at office or workshop, the constables went out for three or four hour stretches of duty, walking monotonously around some gasometer, or standing all night under a railway arch. Men of all classes mingled, spending the long nights in talk: the baronet and the waiter, the titled actor and the pawnbroker's clerk were actual combinations. Sometimes they had to control riots; often they went out in air raids.

The New Army leaves for France: enthusiasm for the war was still high in 1915.

For middle-class women, there were all kinds of voluntary organizations to join: Tipperary Clubs to help soldiers' wives, refugees' funds, prisoners' funds, soldiers' canteens, clubs to help the wounded, war economy leagues. Many women went to help at once in the new war hospitals. Unlucky schoolboys found themselves used for bandaging practice. The knitting mania was part of this first fashionable effort. Women all over Britain made waistcoats, gas helmets, comforters, mitts, body belts, gloves. "We knitted at theatres, in trains and trams, in parks and parlours, in the intervals of eating in restaurants, of serving in canteens," wrote Mrs. Peel in *How we Lived Then*. "It was soothing to our nerves to knit, and comforting to think that the results of our labours might save some man something of hardship and misery. . ." Jessie Pope, the popular "poet," who wrote for the *Daily Mail*, even invented a poem about knitting.

> "Soldier lad, on the sodden ground,
>   Sailor lad, on the seas
> Can't you hear a little clicketty sound,
> Stealing across on the breeze?
> It's the knitting needles singing their tune
>   As they twine the khaki or blue,
> Thousands and thousands and thousands strong,
>   Tommy and Jack for you."

Flag days were a novel, if overworked, idea. Women sold small paper flowers on the streets to collect for various funds. All this dutiful activity among the middle class gave suburban life a new look. There were more women and fewer men on rush hour stations; golf courses were virtually deserted, though oddly trampled by the boots of Kitchener's Army; entertaining, social visiting and afternoon bridge parties or shopping trips to London had been replaced by "a great fervour of work and organization." It was patriotic to do without gardeners, gamekeepers, chauffeurs, even servants. As the butcher's boy had disappeared, the business man now carried home half a ham from the shops himself, hoping his friends wouldn't meet him; his wife crept out to clean the brass name plate on the gate, and hoped the neighbours weren't looking. It was the beginning of the end of the age of the servant.

War Industry

British industry was ill-prepared for war. Her chemical industry was small, and vital products for weapons, such as ball bearings and optical devices, had been imported from Germany before 1914. An enormous effort was required to provide Britain with war material.

The deadlock on the Western Front brought new urgency to the need to provide for the mighty "war of machines." The British battle failures at Neuve Chapelle in March, and at Aubers Ridge in May, were blamed on a shortage of shells: in the controversy-stirring words of the *Daily Mail* correspondent, Colonel Repington: ". . . the want of an unlimited supply of high explosives was a fatal bar to our success." A combination of problems had kept British shell production to a mere 700 a day in the first months of the war (Germany and France were producing 250,000 shells daily). Lord Kitchener, in charge of Army supply,

The Knitting Mania: a *Punch* satire.

Middle class women were keen supporters of the war effort.

insisted on high standards of production, only giving contracts to a handful of firms. At the same time his own appeal for volunteers for his New Armies had already taken a quarter of the employees of vital war industries concerned with explosives, coal, metals and engineering. Even a large firm like Vickers was soon hopelessly unable to fulfil its massive new orders, despite issuing special badges to its workers to protect them from white feathers. There were problems with trades unions, too. There were protests about "dilution," – the use of unskilled workers or women to replace craftsmen and jealously-guarded trade union restricted practices.

A propaganda poster asking everyone to contribute to the war.

Are **YOU** in this?

The "scandal of the shells" contributed to the fall of Herbert Asquith's Liberal Government in May. It was replaced by a coalition of Liberal and Conservative, still under Asquith's leadership. David Lloyd-George, the former Chancellor of the Exchequer, who had already shown great tact and skill in negotiations with trades unions, became Minister of Munitions. Using his organizing genius he built up a Ministry of 65,000 staff, controlling three million workers in thousands of munitions factories throughout the country. Local munitions committees gave out orders to existing firms, large and small, or set up entirely new factories. In quiet country districts, buildings sprang up with astonishing speed. By 1918, the Ministry, following the slogan, "Work! Work! turn out shells!" was able to match the Artillery's gigantic appetite. There was spectacular progress. The annual production of heavy shells in the year 1914–15 was accomplished in four days in 1916; machine-gun production increased sixteen-fold, heavy gun production six-fold. Lloyd George persuaded the conservative Army to accept vital new war winning weapons: the machine gun, the Stokes-mortar, and the supreme British invention, the tank.

The Munitions of War Act of July 1915 laid down rules for an efficient industry. It was quite a revolutionary plan: it attempted to ban strikes in munition work; workers were forbidden to move jobs without a leaving certificate from their employers; trades unions' restricted practices were suspended. Special Munitions courts were to consider disputes. In return for concessions from the workers, profits were supposedly limited, though a crop of war profiteers, "hard faced men who did well out of the war," could not be prevented.

Lloyd George himself toured his factories, inspiring effort with his

famous gifts as a public speaker. The most troublesome areas were South Wales and "Red" Clydeside in Scotland. The socialist shop stewards particularly resented the leaving certificate, seeing it as the start of "industrial conscription." Continual strikes forced the measure to be withdrawn in 1917. Thereafter the threat of the call-up was used to keep a man in the industry. Lloyd George could handle the Welshmen but was barracked in Scotland, despite eloquent promises: "Workers, may I make one appeal to you? Lift up your eyes above the mist of suspicion and distrust. Rise to the heights of the great opportunity now before you. If you do, you will emerge after this war is over into a future which has been the dream of many a great leader!"

Rising wages were enough to avoid too many strikes; indeed, there were fewer disputes in 1915 than in any year since 1910. Workers began to enjoy new affluence. "The sun of industrial prosperity" began to shine. The production boom brought labour shortage, and papers were crammed with advertisements appealing for workers of every kind. Tramps and vagrant unemployed disappeared: "The war had gathered up the fringes of humanity and ravelled them into its wonderful garment," wrote Harold Owen.

One of Lloyd George's measures to stimulate productivity still sur-

The mighty war effort to provide munitions.

Drunkenness, an enemy of war production, was cut by strict new laws governing drinking hours.

vives today: restricted drinking hours. Excessive liquor consumption and absenteeism due to hangovers was affecting the war effort. In several speeches, the Minister denounced drunkenness: "Drink is doing us more damage in the war than all the German submarines put together;" "The men who drink at home are murdering the men in the trenches;" "We are fighting Germany, Austria and drink . . ." Under D.O.R.A. (liquor control) regulations, public houses were now closed in the mornings and afternoons, "treating" (that is buying drinks for other people, especially soldiers) was forbidden, beer was reduced in strength and made more expensive, spirits became luxuries, which were hard to obtain especially in munition areas. Drunkenness, a pre-war characteristic of British life, now became a limited social problem. Convictions for drinking fell from 156,000 in 1913 to 77,000 in 1916. Consumption was halved in Britain by 1918. George V himself took the "King's Pledge" to abstain from alcohol, and newspapers began publishing recipes for non-alcoholic drinks.

Women and "The Right to Serve"

A novelty of Lloyd George's munitions factories was to be the use of female labour. On 17th July, 1915, a huge procession of women was organized by the former suffragette organizations, which had struggled so violently in pre-war years to win women the vote. In 1914 they had decided to dedicate themselves to the war effort. Macdonagh watched their rally: "It included a 'Pageant of the Allies' which was headed by a young women wearing a Grecian robe of white fringed with gold, and carrying a trophy composed of the flags of the nations at war with Germany . . . A girl in white carrying an armful of roses represented England." The intention was to impress Lloyd George, who was watching, with women's willingness to contribute to the war effort. "There were numerous banners with inscriptions such as 'Women's Battle Cry is work, work, work' and 'Shells made by a wife may save her husband's life!'" Lloyd George promised to help, noting "this procession will educate public opinion."

Although there was still resentment from male trade unionists, who feared cheap labour and "dilution," the public was now willing to accept women workers. Declining public services, delays, rising costs due to labour shortages made them inevitable. For women, there was the necessity to earn their own living; for the government, there was pressure to free more men for war.

Thousands of women entered commerce, banks and government offices. "No woman worker is in greater demand than the shorthand typist," commented the *Daily Mail*, which went on to list the new occupations for women, many of them hard physical tasks. Although such work had been the normal lot of women throughout the centuries, the newspapers, short of solid news, made it a sensation. Most significant for the war effort was the employment of women in munitions factories, where their deft fingers excelled in fuse-making. To be a "munitionette" became something of a craze, even among "society" girls. By the end of 1915, there were three women for every man in munitions. Despite this, their pay was less than half that of men.

Women took over many of the jobs that the men left behind when they marched off to the Front.

49

Wartime advertisements.

A Changing World

During 1915, the perceptive *Times* home correspondent toured British
towns and cities noting the changes brought by war. London's traffic was
as thick as usual; cars and buses and thousands of commercial carts still
flowed through the streets. All seemed as usual but for the khaki uniforms
and recruiting notices. Only at night did the blackout bring a severe
change. The public never seemed tired of walking to and fro, looking up
to where the search-lights wheeled endlessly across the threatening sky.
The East End was particularly depressing in the gloom, "the faded shop
windows and frowsy house fronts hopelessly uninviting." However,
"every by-street [had] its link with the New Army," and a new patriotic
pride sustained the crowded poor. New clothing and equipment-
makers' factories sprang up. Even ordinary houses became workshops in
the boom.

Brighton, like most seaside resorts on the South and East coasts, was
"veiled in deep darkness." By a stroke of the imagination, the Brighton
Pavilion, with its domes and minarets, had been turned into a hospital
for Indian soldiers. Its grounds were full of "dusky and turbaned oriental
warriors." The seaside pleasure-boats had lost their familiar names – *My
Pretty Jane, The Prairie-Flower, Old Bob Ridley* – and had been grimly
numbered for military identification. Liverpool was bustling with its
American trade, although most of the great ships, taken over by the
government, were now painted black or slate-grey. Later they appeared
in fantastic dazzle-patterns to deceive submarines. Hotels were full and
ablaze with lights, as the city was as yet safe from Zeppelins. Birmingham
was equally careless, its great shopping streets full of light and colour.
Here the demands of the Army brought industrial boom: "The city was
a great community with its coat off and its sleeves rolled up." The war
effort in Leeds gave "a terrific working day in hot and noisy mills . . . The
dividing line between day and night is so obliterated that despair fills the
heart of many a 'knocker-up,' the man with the long pole who taps at
workers' windows to waken them for work." Sheffield was visible from
far away by the blast furnaces that threw "a blood-red glare on the screen
of night." The undergraduates of Oxford and Cambridge had been
among the keenest of Kitchener volunteers. Therefore "at 11 or noon,
the streets are not now a-flutter with gowns hurrying up to lectures: at
1 o'clock, the groups in the gateways are scanty or none . . . By night
and by day, there is a hush over the colleges, where set upon set of empty
rooms seem to stare at the empty quadrangle in surprise . . ." In the
countryside the loss of men was particularly remarkable. H. W. Wilson
remembered, in his *Great War,* how "The fields and farms and inns were
emptied. A quiet as of a house in which the dead lie unburied brooded
over the land . . . and in almost every window was the name of one who
was fighting for freedom, or whose fight had ended for ever."

3 1916

"On Sussex hills today
  Women stand and hear
The guns at work alway,
  Horribly, terribly clear . . ."
    Ivor Gurney, "Rumours of Wars"

Conscription

BEFORE THE WAR, the idea of conscription had seemed "The very symbol of tyranny," totally opposed to British ideals of liberty of the individual. As the supply of volunteer recruits declined, a chorus of protest arose against the "inequality of sacrifice" being made for the war effort. A woman who had lost her husband and son wrote angrily to the press complaining about "young fellows lolling about and enjoying themselves" in London. She expressed the thoughts of thousands of others. "Probably there are very few of our readers who do not know of at least one case of men who should be serving," commented the *Daily Mail*. Older men resented idle younger men: even Arnold Bennett found himself thinking: "When one sees young men idling in the lanes on Sunday, one thinks 'Why are they not at the war?'" The Derby Scheme of 1915 having failed, Prime Minister Asquith could now claim that voluntarism had failed.

Under the first Military Service Act of January, 1916, which introduced compulsion, all single men between 18 and 41 were "deemed to have enlisted." The Second Military Service Act of May, 1916 included married men, too, in the Army net. Every fit man was to serve unless specially exempted. This satisfied the "slacker" hunters for some time, although strangely the flow of men into the Army during 1916 was actually half that under the voluntary system.

Conscientious Objectors

Most criticism of the Military Service Acts was directed at a particular clause allowing exemptions based on a "conscientious objection to the undertaking of combatant service." Men whose personal principles did not allow them to support the war were to be called before Local Tribunals set up in all districts throughout the country to consider cases.

There was a howl of protest about the "conshies" or "Cuthberts." They were, according to the popular press, "sickly idealists," "flimsy sentimentalists," "pasty faces," "curs," "anarchists." They suffered from "fatty degeneration of the soul." They were men "with as much pluck and brains as the rabbit and as much conscience as the skunk." The *Daily Express* led the campaign against them: "New name for the slackers – conscientious objectors. It is perfectly certain that every coward and slacker in the land will find his conscience forbids him to fight." Horatio Bottomley's *John Bull* was another bitter opponent: "The

Opposite. Conscription of all adult males for the Services was introduced in early 1916. From *Punch*, captioned "The New Edge."

53

"This little pig stayed at home." The "Conshie" derided in the magazine *John Bull*.

A cartoon protesting against conscription, published in the pacifist paper *Workers' Dreadnought*.

"GOT HIM"

conscientious objector is a fungus growth – a human toadstool – which should be uprooted without further delay." The harsh, crude resentment of the exemption clause is best summed up in an anonymous "poem" written by a "soldier";

> "The best place for such moral objectors
> Is a land where the climate is hot,
> And into the brimstone of Hades
> Good soldiers would throw in the lot.
> For the man who is born of a nation
> Who shrinks in the hour of her strife,
> In a contest for freedom's salvation,
> No longer is worthy of life."

Some, like the Quakers, stood against the war on religious grounds: "All war is utterly incompatible with the plain precepts of our Divine Lord and Law Giver." There were also socialists, who believed in international brotherhood among working men. These two strands of opposition met in the two objector societies, the Union of Democratic Control (U.D.C.) and the No-Conscription Fellowship (N.C.F.). Their manifesto said: "The destruction of our fellow men appals us; we cannot assist in the cutting off of one generation from life's opportunities... We deny the right of any Government to make slaughter of our fellows a bounden duty." Their meetings were broken up by demonstrators, notably Dominion soldiers, who jeered, threw stink-bombs and rushed the platforms, to the satisfaction of the *Daily Express*, who announced "utter rout of the Pro-Germans."

The tribunals, consisting of local tradesmen and worthies, mostly elderly men, sometimes with a woman representative, always with a dominant soldier spokesman, began their work in March. Cases were elaborately detailed in local papers, so that the community could apply its own pressures to individuals. The tribunals gave scant sympathy to the objectors' principles. Their interviews were unimaginative: Their favourite question was "What would you do if a German attacked your mother or your sister?" They granted few exemptions, guided by the government's dull promise to make the path of the Conscientious Objector a "hard one." Most objectors agreed to assist the war effort in non-combatant service, in forestry, road making or labour camps. The Quaker ambulance units contained some of the bravest men at the

A group of Conscientious Objectors.

Postcards about Conscientious Objectors, probably printed by friends of imprisoned C.O.s outside prison and sold in aid of the prisoners' dependents.

Front and they won many medals. There were, however, about 1,500 "absolutists," who refused to help in any way. In such a case, the man was "deemed to have enlisted," and could then be arrested and taken to military camp, where he found himself under Army Law. Thus refusing to obey an officer's order could mean a court martial. About 6,000 men were imprisoned, and seventy died from their treatment there. Others were bullied by brutal N.C.O.'s – one man had to stand for days in a waterlogged pit in the ground. Some men were even shipped to France and threatened with the death penalty for desertion. This was "British Prussianism," as the N.C.F. called it, and its excesses brought scandal. "Where are we drifting?" asked the *Daily News*.

The objectors won sympathy, where their protest was based on sincere principles. Michael Macdonagh attended a Tribunal session in London and saw a young man with long hair and beard, a member of a religious sect known as the "Israelites." He was opposed to the taking of life from man or animal. In answer to the usual crude questioning, he said, "I rely upon the injunction 'thou shalt not kill!'" "Are not men of this type," concluded Macdonagh, "instead of being cowards and knaves, as some of us regard them, often the stuff of which the saviours of mankind are made?"

56

H. M. Prison, W Wood Scrub

2 . 10 . 1916

Dear Father

I am now in this Prison, and am in Usual *health.*

If I behave well, I shall be allowed to write ~~another~~ *letter about*

8 Weeks *and to receive a reply, but no reply is*

allowed to this. May Sentence es 6 months

Signature— Harold F. Bing

Register No. 1216

Two letters sent from prison by a Conscientious Objector, Harold Bing. *Left.* The usual first letter which a prisoner was allowed to send. *Right.* A letter written on toilet paper by Mr. Bing and smuggled out of prison. It is addressed to the Croydon branch of the No Conscription Fellowship.

The name of the prison (Wormwood Scrubs), the destination and writer's signature were deleted in case the letter was seized by the authorities en route.

To the ████ N.C.F.— 13.12.16

Heartiest Greetings! Keep the Flag flying outside! We in here are in the highest spirits, and are determined to stand firm to the end, come what may. In the cause of Freedom it is a small sacrifice temporarily to ~~give~~ give up one's personal liberty. After all it is only our bodily freedom that we relinquish: our spirits are far freeer than the spirits of those who accept the yoke of militarism. Surely the Cause for which we strive is worthy; and in a worthy cause no sacrifice is too great.

Though separated from you in the body, Comrades, we are one with you in spirit; one in the fight for freedom; one in the cause of international peace & brotherhood. May no factions divide us till our purpose is achieved.— And now farewell & God be with you till we meet again!

N.B. Written with a needle & a little ink in the lid of

Even after the Somme slaughter, the peace advocates won no popular support in 1916. Sylvia Pankhurst, who worked in the East End of London and contributed to a pacifist paper *Workers' Dreadnought*, found hostile crowds of women, who demanded only revenge for dead sons: "Saddest of all were the degraded; the starved and the shabby, who rushed intoxicated from the public houses, shrieking with hideous epithets, 'Fight on to Victory!' demanding that the entire German population should be 'wiped out'! Sometimes they would attempt a tipsy war dance in the midst of our crowd."

A well-known popular response to suggestions of a negotiated peace was the letter of the "Little Mother" published in the *Morning Post:* "We women, who demand to be heard, will tolerate no such cry as 'Peace! Peace!' where there is no peace . . . Send the Pacifists to us and we shall soon show them . . . There is only one temperature for the women of the British race, and that is white heat . . . We women pass on the human ammunition of 'only sons' to fill up the gaps, so that when the 'Common Soldier' looks back before going 'over the top' he may see the women of the British race on his heels, reliable, dependent, uncomplaining . . ." So popular was this letter that it was specially published as a pamphlet, and praised as showing "the loftiest ideal, tempered with courage and the most sublime sacrifice."

D

57

Below. Women at work in a shell factory, Such work was very dangerous – the picture on the right shows the aftermath of an explosion at Silvertown munitions factory in 1917.

Women at Work

The coming of conscription increased the employment of women. They were now seen everywhere in daily life; at the wheel of motor cars and vans, handling the reins of horses, collecting tickets at underground stations, running hotel lifts, even serving as "waiters" in the exclusively male West End Clubs. Public favourites were the "conductorettes" on buses and trams. "I had quite a thrill," said Macdonagh, "the first time one said to me as I mounted her moving bus, 'Hold tight, please Sir.'" The first "land-girls," who went to help on farms, shocked the countryside with their bold adoption of male-style dress for their work. As housemaids flocked into the factories, numbers of women, as many as 400,000 during the whole war, abandoned domestic service, most of them never to return.

The girls of the munitions factories were the most discussed in the national press. The writer, Hall Caine, in an article, called them, "A brave camaraderie. An old Roman writer tells how the wives ground the swords of their warrior husbands and exhorted them to deeds of valour. What else are these daughters of Britain doing?" Many were, in fact, soldiers' wives and were therefore sternly motivated. A notice in Woolwich Arsenal read:

"Motive for work: patriotism. A munition worker is as important as the soldier in the trenches, and on her his life depends.

Aim: Output. Anyone who limits this is a traitor to sweethearts, husbands and brothers fighting . . ."

The dangers of the work only gradually overcame female vanities. Uniform trousers slowly replaced skirts, caps and then short "bobbed" hair replaced long tresses, which were easily caught in the machines. Despite this, many girls clung to "a complete unsuitability of boots." Arnold Bennett was fascinated to watch a girl delicately rolling a nine-

Are **YOU** in this?

TAKE UP THE SWORD OF JUSTICE

Left. A poster calling on the whole country to join in the war effort.

Below. Many women were employed in the highly dangerous munitions industry.

Bottom. The sinking of the liner *Lusitania* by a German submarine inspired this poster.

THESE WOMEN ARE DOING THEIR BIT

LEARN TO MAKE MUNITIONS

Overleaf. Ambulances at Charing Cross, by J. Hodgson Lobley.

A display of First World War ephemera – an embroidered postcard sent from the Front, and flags and badges which were sold on the streets in aid of various funds.

inch shell with her foot, her fashionable boot showing beneath her over-all. "These things, happily, will peep out."

There were more terrible dangers, not so easily ignored. Despite the use of masks or respirators and unpleasant facial grease, the fumes from T.N.T. turned the girls' faces a hideous yellow. These girls were called "the canaries." The historian, Caroline Playne, saw a train full of them at a Midland station. They were "Amazonian beings, bereft of all charm of appearance, clothed anyhow, skin stained a yellow-brown even to the roots of their dishevelled hair by the awful stuff they handled."Women varnishing aeroplane wings were overcome by the toxic fumes; they were seen lying sick in rows outside the workshops. Even more perilous were the "monkey machines," in which a heavy weight was dropped to compress explosive into shell cases. A seventeen year old girl, for example, was the only survivor of four workers, when a shell exploded in the machines. She lost a leg and was terribly mutilated by flying metal. Lloyd George had strong admiration for the "munitionettes" working in his factories. Shortly after several women had been killed in an explosion while they were screwing shell fuses, his representative found women busily at work in the blood-stained hut where the accident happened.

A more extensive disaster, like the huge explosion at the Silvertown ammunition factory in London early in 1917, was fortunately rare. Macdonagh witnessed the blast and was convinced it was some new giant German bomb. The sky was lit by a golden glow, then a high column of yellow flame arose, which changed to a sunset-like variety of violet, indigo, blue, green, yellow, orange and red. A terrific explosion, heard fifty miles away, shattered the air, while a vibrating, earthquake tremor ran through the city. A square mile of buildings was razed to the ground. Two thousand people were made homeless. Sixty-nine more were killed and four hundred and fifty injured, including many women. Such were the dangers women faced as they "ground the swords of their soldier husbands."

However, many working class women found pleasure in new inde-pendence, after dead-end marriages in which they were treated as inferiors. "I'd never known what it was to be a free woman before," one of them told Mrs. Peel. Their new affluence brought them a new look: powder and make-up became common; silk stockings were bought by working class shell-girls, and they smoked openly in public. The short skirt (still below the knee) was the symbol of the new woman. Mac-donagh saw the change in the City of London where "thousands of girls are earning their living in city offices . . . Had petticoats and long skirts and the fashion of hips, busts and narrow waists continued, this perhaps would have been impossible." The short skirts allowed greater mobility and were therefore, like the land girls' trousers, a necessity. However, the conservative press disapproved: a hem six inches off the ground was "extravagantly short . . . revealing the feet and ankles and even more of the stockings – ." The *Daily Mail* attacked them: "Just now our young and pretty girls are pushing the craze for short skirts to the utmost limit, but even now these ultra-remarkable models are regarded with sus-picion by women of good taste."

There was another reason for short skirts – sheer needs of economy.

War economy dress: simpler fashions were forced on women partly by war work, partly by growing shortages of materials.

War fashions – the new shorter skirts.

63

Anxious women scan the papers for news from the Front.

There were even exhibitions of War Economy dress, designed to save material. While working girls showed off new finery, it was the fashion among the middle classes to dress plainly, even shabbily. Articles about the making of chic blouses and dainty negligees were replaced by instructions for making chest protectors, flannel gas masks, operation shirts and special bandages.

War was a stimulant to better industrial working conditions, especially for women. The realization of the link between output and the welfare of the worker brought this social advance. Several Government reports on efficiency in the munitions factories noted that meals were eaten in the workroom, that there were no proper washing facilities or rest rooms, that travel was difficult and day shift workers were taking over beds from night shift workers in the inadequate living accommodation put up near new factories. Reforms were rapidly instituted: cheap but good food in canteens, medical rooms and nurses, recreational clubs, proper bedrooms and wash-rooms, even nurseries for women's children. The improvements lasted beyond the war as one of its few benefits. "It is a strange irony," said Lloyd George in 1916, "that the making of weapons of destruction should afford occasion to humanize industry. Yet such has been the case."

64

The Battle of the Somme

Saturday 1st July, 1916 was the notorious first day of the Battle of the Somme, a huge Franco-British effort to break the Western Front. A mighty bombardment of more than a million and a half shells preceded the attack. Throughout the previous week the ominous muttering of the guns had been clearly heard in Britain. The vibration rattled windows at South Coast towns and villages, or was felt even in the floors of buildings in London. In shell factories, the Whitsun holidays had been postponed to provide for the expected victorious "Big Push." However, when thousands of British troops rose from their trenches to attack the German lines, they found the ground littered with unexploded shells, and German machine gunners, emerging from deep dugouts, untouched by the hurricane of fire poured onto their positions, were able to cut down the attackers. Nearly 20,000 British soldiers died on that first day; nearly 40,000 others were seriously wounded. Among the losses were 30,419 New Army men, the eager volunteers of 1914, in action for the first time, whose battalions, two years in the making, were cut to pieces in twelve hours.

British troops go over the top at the terrible Battle of the Somme, July 1916.

The Somme was the largest British land battle since the days of Waterloo. It ground on until November, ending in a sea of mud, the armies having wrested a small devastated piece of occupied France from the enemy. "The long and sombre procession of cruelty and suffering," as Asquith called it (he lost his eldest son there) caused nearly half a million British casualties.

Home interest in the Battle was intense. Almost every family in the land knew someone "on the Somme." Partly out of duty, partly because they did not know, partly because D.O.R.A. forbade gloomy war news, the newspaper correspondents, now grudgingly allowed at the Front by the Army, presented the first day of the Somme as a victory. "The *Observer* was typical. Under a heading, "The Big Push: a great beginning," the editor described "The Sacrifice, the heroism and inspiration of these days . . . For Britain [they] are the most glorious and terrible in our history . . . The New Armies, fighting with a valour and fibre never surpassed by any people, have excelled our best hopes." The pitifully small territorial gains and the heavy losses were disguised. Men were "slightly wounded," losses were "by no means excessive." The fighting proved that "the average Britisher was a better man than the average German. We have 'em cold." Kitchener's men had shown their courage. A *Punch* poem praised them:

A soldier after the Battle of the Somme.

> ". . . from mine and desk and mart,
> Springing to face a task undreamed before,
> Our men, inspired to play their prentice part
> Like soldiers lessoned in the school of war,
>   True to their breed and name,
> Went flawless through the fierce Baptismal flame."

Soldiers wounded from the Battle, "with the mud of the trenches still clinging to them," were given a heroes' welcome. Crowds gathered along the railway lines from Folkestone or Southampton to wave at the frequent ambulance trains. At Charing Cross, excited crowds gathered:

E

A battle victim by a war artist.

"You saw women buying up the street sellers' roses and tossing them into taxis that brought the slightly wounded away." The provinces were equally excited about their "Heroes of the Great Battle," and people lined routes to hospitals pressing flowers and sweets on the wounded.

The Somme Dead

It was not long before the truth about the Somme slaughter began to appear in extensive newspaper columns of casualties. Whole pages were grey with hundreds of names. Suffering in certain towns, where Pals' battalions had been formed, was particularly severe. Complete units had been cut down together before the German trench strongholds. British soldiers coming to the front after the first day had seen these dead, hanging grotesquely on the barbed wire, "like wreckage washed up to a high water mark." They had had the terrible task of clearing the decaying, rat-gnawed bodies, which often fell to pieces in their hands. These were the dead that British families were mourning. Whole streets had drawn blinds. Crowds surrounded council and newspaper offices demanding the truth. At Accrington in Lancashire rumour said that only seven Pals had survived in the town's battalion (in fact, 585 from 700 attackers had become casualties). Local papers began publishing rows of photographs of the dead. In London's East End, pathetic street shrines sprang up, carrying names of local victims, surrounded by flowers and photographs of the Royal family. At the other end of the social scale, many sons of noble families died in this battle. Fifty famous and ancient family names thus became extinct before the end of the war.

Thousands of telegrams, often curtly phrased, brought the bad news to anxious homes. Vera Brittain, then a V.A.D. Nurse, remembered the news of her brother's death: the "sudden loud clattering at the front door knocker that always meant a telegram," the "tearing anguish of suspense" as it was opened. Mrs. Peel recalled the deadly effect of the telegram on a friend, with whom she was playing bridge: "The poor

The grieving wife, holding her dead husband's Victoria Cross. From the *Illustrated London News*.

"Her son's V.C." The King presents the medal to "the mother of a fallen hero." From the *Illustrated London News*.

"Missing." The agonising enquiries at the War Office for those lost in battle. Note the Boy Scout official messenger. From the *Graphic*.

woman's face went white. Her cards fell out of her shaking hands. I thought she was going to faint . . . It was the telegram . . . her son had been killed." After visiting grieving mothers, Michael Macdonagh movingly described their plight. "We can imagine them in their loneliness grieving as they listen to the prattle long ago of their little children who now as boys are lying in graves in France and Flanders . . . They are miserable and rebellious in spirit. You can see their mood in the strained expression of their eyes, denoting unshed tears. Rage is in their hearts at what they regard as the purposeless sacrifice of their sons. Lost! Wasted!" Most bitter anguish was felt by relatives of those declared "missing." They hunted hospitals, wrote to battalions, sought out soldier friends, advertised pitifully in special columns in the newspapers.

Some people sought relief from sorrow in the vogue for spiritualism, in which women tried to contact their dead menfolk "beyond the sun" at seances. Robert Graves, on leave from the Somme, had his night's sleep disturbed at a friend's home, by weird rappings, shrieks and laughter. All sorts of palmists, mediums and crystal gazers were popular. Many frauds were prosecuted after police raids on fortune telling parlours. Charms and mascots were bought by women anxious that their man should be safe in the Front Line. A small pocket New Testament was said to be useful as a protection against bullets, when carried in a breast pocket. For those to whom patriotic martyrdom provided no consolation, religion offered relief. Sentimental versifiers like John Oxenham, with his "helpful verse for these dark days of war," suggested divine rewards for dead soldiers:

> "Unnamed at times, at times unknown,
> Our graves lie thick beyond the seas;
> Unnamed but not of Him unknown;
> He knows! He sees!"

The Battle of the Somme, a brutal struggle of attrition, killed the first enthusiasm for the war. After this battle, the Front-line "out there" in France became more terrible and mysterious. The novelist H. M. Tomlinson compared it to the dark, sinister maze on King Minos's Crete, where lived the monstrous Minotaur, to which the Greeks were compelled to send each year the very best of their young people: "France was as dark as that, though so near to us."

The Soldier on Leave

To the trench soldier, England, or "Blighty," was a longed-for haven. On the leave boat he saw the white cliffs, then, as the R.F.C. pilot V. M.

The cartoons of Bruce Bairnsfather, a serving officer at the Front, were widely reproduced in magazines and on postcards. *Left.* "A Winter's Tale." *Right.* "A.D. 19**(?). 'I see the war babies battalion is a-comin' out.'"

"Back to Blighty." War-worn soldiers return home on leave. Published in the *Graphic*.

Yeates recalled in his book *Winged Victory*, the "wandering lanes, hedged and ditched; casual, opulent beauty, trees heavy with fulfilment . . . Green hedgerows again between green meadows and cornfields where reapers were busy." Kent countryside was exquisite for one who had seen the Somme wastelands. In London the leave soldiers, said Macdonagh, "looked more like strange beings from another world, fully equipped as they were, and stained with the mud of the trenches." Britain looked equally strange to them, especially the war madness running wild everywhere looking for some pseudo-military outlet. The sentimental "Tommy" of the journalists puzzled and angered the soldier. R. H. Tawney, then a wounded New Army sergeant, wrote derisively to the *Nation* magazine: "This Tommy is a creature at once ridiculous and disgusting. He is represented as invariably 'cheerful' and revelling in the 'excitement' of war, of finding 'sport' in killing other men, or hunting Germans out of dugouts as a terrier hunts rats . . . We are depicted as merry assassins rejoicing in the opportunity of a 'scrap' . . . exulting in the duty of turning human beings into lumps of disfigured clay . . . Of your soldier's internal life, the sensation of taking part in a game played by monkeys and organized by lunatics, you realize, I think, nothing." With the Somme began the feeling of alienation between the fighting man and civilians so typical of the war. "Broadly speaking," wrote F. H. Keeling, another New Army man, "the English either volunteer for this hell or else sit down and grow fat on big money at home."

Wandering the streets of London, the soldier could notice the changes brought by war. Its huge cost was beginning to take effect. Recruiting posters were now replaced by economy appeals: "Spend less; Save more!," "Buy only War Savings Certificates." People looked shabbier,

A soldier and his wife at the station. Drawing by Frank Reynolds, from *Punch*.

69

A troop train arrives at a London terminus.

A Tommy on leave, still dressed in his strange trench clothes, asks the way in London.

especially men. Trousers with baggy knees and frayed edges showed that you were "doing your bit." The top hat, symbol of extravagance, was disappearing. Following government restriction of petrol, there were fewer cars and buses. Horse-drawn vehicles began to re-appear. The nostalgic jingle of the hansom cab was heard again. Four-wheelers, the "growler" carriages of Victorian times, were seen, "brought out from the dark cobwebbed corner of some stable, with appropriately ancient drivers." Shop fronts looked dingy, lacking coats of fresh paint, due to wartime economies. The once bright flower-beds in the Royal Parks were now grass-grown, and the lake in St. James's Park drained (its distinctive shape might help to guide Zeppelins) and new temporary Government buildings were erected on the site. There were more and more of these ugly sheds in the parks as the war went on.

The streets were full of soldiers. Wounded men were being driven about with their nurses to see the sights, and Dominion soldiers, "tall lean fellows, springy in their walk, wearing broad-brimmed khaki hats, gay with feathers," attracted the notice. Some of the colour had departed from London life. The street musicians, like the German bands that had toured the country in pre-war summers, the hurdy-gurdy man with his barrel-organ, the cornet player by the public house, had all disappeared. So had "those benefactors of the London night," the hot potato man, the roast chestnut man, the midnight coffee stall. The soldiers on guard in Whitehall had lost their scarlet jackets, gleaming breastplates and plumed helmets, and were now in drab khaki. London statues, and the famous tombs in Westminster Abbey, were shrouded in sandbags. Old stained glass was removed from church windows. Big Ben, on the Houses of Parliament, was forbidden to strike. The very shape of the day was different: the new "summer time" put clocks forward an hour to

A soldier on leave arrives home, to be greeted by his mother.

give war work extra daylight.

In a dreary economy move, several large London museums and galleries were closed, despite protests that they might benefit men on leave. Their buildings were to be used for war work. What, it was asked, had "deciphering hieroglyphics" or "cataloguing microlepidoptera" to do with the war effort? The staff thus freed joined the Army. Madame Tussaud's Waxwork Exhibition remained open, however, displaying "life-like portrait models" of John Travers Cornwall, V.C., the boy seaman, who died doing his duty beside his ship's gun at the Battle of Jutland (fought in May 1916), and Captain Fryatt, a merchant marine officer executed by the Germans after he tried to ram a submarine.

If "culture" was frowned upon, pleasure was booming. Hundreds of night clubs opened in London. Theatres and music-halls were crowded. The great popular successes were *Chu Chin Chow* at His Majesty's, *Peg O'My Heart* at the Globe, *The Bing Boys* at the Alhambra, with George Robey, the comedian, singing "If you were the only girl in the world." War plays enjoyed a surprising vogue. In the music-halls, coarse Hun-hunting songs mingled with old sentimental favourites. Soldiers saw these shows and took the poignant songs back with them to France, to sing on the march or to play endlessly on scratchy records in their trench dugouts. Not everyone approved of this restless search for pleasure. A General wrote angrily to the *Morning Post:* "I am convinced that our gallant sailors and soldiers themselves . . . would prefer performances which, while cheerful and inspiring, appealed to the best side of their patriotic natures, and not exhibitions of scantily dressed girls and songs of doubtful character . . ."

At the end of leave, the great London termini, Charing Cross and Victoria, were scenes of leave-taking. Siegfried Sassoon, in *Memoirs of an Infantry Officer,* remembered the station partings: "Some sauntered away with assumed unconcern; they chattered and smiled. Others

OPTIMIST. PESSIMIST. PLUTOCRAT. SLACKERS. RUMOUR-MONGER.

Wartime types caricatured in *Punch* by Frank Reynolds.

The trench hero relates his experiences. In reality, the soldier often found it hard to communicate with people at home. From the *Sphere*.

hurried past me with a crucified look; I noticed a well-dressed woman biting her gloved fingers; her eyes stared fixedly. She was returning alone to a silent house on a fine Sunday afternoon." While trains full of fresh troops returning to battle steamed out, hospital trains full of shattered victims glided ominously in to take their places.

War and the Cinema

The cinema was well established as the "poor man's theatre" by 1916. There were some three thousand cinemas in Britain, attracting twenty million attendances a week. Films were short, a programme being made up of "two reelers." Charlie Chaplin was the chief attraction.

Most cinema-going in wartime was escapism, for audiences seeking entertainment and excitement as an antidote to an increasingly dreary wartime world. However, the government soon learned the power of cinema propaganda. In a film like *England's Call* (1914) great national figures of the past – Raleigh, Wellington, Nelson, General Gordon and others – left their portrait frames to ask for recruits. In *Britain Prepared* (1914), there were glimpses of Kitchener's Army in training and the Grand Fleet at sea. The captions for the silent films were in the current style: "We show you the brave men who went with throbbing hearts and tuneful lips to face the slaughter and carnage" or "The noblest manhood of our race responded to the divine impulse." Some films were propaganda against the enemy. "Once a Hun always a Hun" showed two brutal German soldiers attacking a woman in Belgium. Then they were seen as commercial travellers in Britain after the war. Their made-in-Germany goods were rejected by the village shopkeeper, with the final slogan: "There can be no trading with these people after the war." "Tags" became popular: brief films advising you to "Buy War Loans" or "Save Coal" were flashed on the screen during the programme.

Station leave-takings as men return to the nightmare of the Front.

Queues for a war play in London. The war reached a height of popularity in 1916.

Above. The cinema became immensely popular during the war. Here, Charlie Chaplin, best loved star of the era, appears in *Shoulder Arms,* a comic film about the trenches.

Right. The Battle of the Ancre was one of several documentary films which showed the British public some of the reality of war, instead of the often sentimental distortions of the illustrated magazines.

The official documentary films like *The Battle of the Somme* (1916) caused the greatest stir. The Somme film, which appeared in August, although it was only a fairly crude series of incidents, filmed in the first week of the fighting, created a sensation. Families everywhere in Britain flocked to see their men in action: 250,000 bookings were made by cinemas throughout the country. The King advised, "the public should see this picture," and Lloyd George exhorted, "Be up and doing! See that this picture, which is in itself the epic of self sacrifice and gallantry, reaches everyone. Herald the deeds of our brave men to the ends of the earth. This is your duty!"

In London the critics noted the significance of the new vision of battle, as great a step in the presentation of war to the civilian as the celebrated photographs of the Crimea or the American Civil War in the previous century. The *Nation* reporter was struck by the reality of the scenes: "There is the thing itself; this is what men really did . . . That was the look on their faces as they went to death, there is the cigarette still smoking. What would we not give for a glimpse of the thin line springing to advance when Wellington waved his hat at Waterloo." Packed houses watched the film. In Cambridge, the local critic was cheered: "One comes from *The Battle of the Somme* filled with a new pride, a refreshed optimism, conscious of coming victory, calm in the sure knowledge that the German eagle has matched its strength with the British Lion and failed." He liked the piano music provided for the silent film: "Stirring war songs are played as the troops sway past on their march into battle and, a moment later, as the dead heroes are seen lying in the field, the 'Flowers of the Forest' is most feelingly rendered." The next official film, *Battle of the Ancre* was equally popular, with its glimpses of the much-discussed new "tanks" that had appeared in battle during September. By 1918, the Ministry of Information's documentaries had made a careful record of war in the trenches, allowing the public to see reality, instead of the sentimental distortions of the magazine illustrators.

A still from the *Battle of the Somme* showing Kitchener's Volunteer Army on the eve of battle.

The End of the Zeppelins

The Zeppelins were causing panic in Britain: holiday resorts in the West Country advertised prominently as refuges for the nervous; city dwellers showed a new interest in the phases of the moon; and magazines published charts showing the dreaded moonless nights ("Zeppelin black" wrote D. H. Lawrence) when the raiders came. As the airships approached, the crash of distant guns silenced the threatened towns, police whistles and sirens rent the air. People became anxious and hurried in their movements, and the rush for shelter began. For those brave enough to watch, there was fascinating beauty in the spectacle. In *Kangaroo* D. H. Lawrence painted a memorable picture of air raids on London: "There, in the sky, like some god vision, a Zeppelin, and the searchlights catching it . . . then losing it, so that only a strange drumming came down out of the sky where the searchlights tangled their feelers. There it was again, high, high, high, tiny, pale . . . And the crashes of guns, and the awful hoarseness of shells bursting in the city. Then gradually quiet. And from Parliament Hill, a great red glare below, near St. Pauls. Something

THE CAUTIOUS.

THE ABANDONED.

THE ABSENT-MINDED.

Assorted costumes for watching Zeppelins at night. Drawn by Frank Reynolds, published in *Punch*.
Opposite. Spectators watch a burning Zeppelin.

ablaze in the city . . .''

Although the Germans used larger, faster "Super Zeppelins" in 1916, that could fly higher, their doom was already sealed. An explosive bullet had been invented to set fire to their gas-bags. Armed with these, even the ramshackle BE2C aeroplanes, flying to defend London, brought spectacular destruction to the raiders during the Autumn of 1916.

On 2nd September came the first omen of success for London's air defences. A wooden-framed Shutte-Lanz, one of a fleet of sixteen attacking airships, was caught in search-lights and set ablaze by Second-Lieutenant Leefe-Robinson of the R.F.C. A huge fire lit up the surrounding landscape as the wreck sank to earth. Twenty miles away, it was said, people could see "to read their newspapers." In the last blaze of white fire, the dome of St. Pauls, the towers of Westminster Abbey, and the silver Thames stood out in vivid illumination. Wild cheering and shouting broke out across the city. The delighted pilot, who was to win the Victoria Cross for his exploit, shot off all his Very signal lights and looped the loop. The huge blazing wreck, trailing a tail of sparks like a comet, crashed in Cuffley, north of London. The German dead were given a military burial, although an angry woman threw eggs during the funeral of "the baby-killers."

This was only the beginning. On 23rd September, the Zeppelins returned. One, after starting "the most dangerous fires of the war" in Thames-side warehouses, was hit by artillery fire, and, leaking badly, limped only as far as Mersea Island at the mouth of the Thames. The crew, having set fire to their ship, began to walk to the coast to find a boat, but were arrested by a gallant policeman. Another Zeppelin went down in flames. The report of the R.F.C. pilot makes dramatic reading: "I could distinctly see the propellers revolving, and the airship was manoeuvring to avoid the search-light beams." His explosive bullets set the envelope ablaze: a dull red glow spread across the hull turning to white hot flame. The tremendous spectacle provided a focus for the British passion for revenge against the raiders. Michael Macdonagh was walking home from the office: "I was crossing Blackfriars Bridge, when my attention was attracted by frenzied cries of 'Oh, she's hit!' . . . The Zeppelin drifted perpendicularly in the darkened sky, a gigantic pyramid of flames, red and orange, like a ruined star falling slowly to earth. Its glare lit up the streets and gave a ruddy tint even to the water of the Thames . . . When at last the doomed airship vanished from sight, there arose a shout, the like of which I have never heard in London before – a hoarse shout of mingled execration, triumph and joy . . . it was London's 'Te Deum' for another crowning deliverance."

When daylight came, crowds gathered at "The Place." Macdonagh joined the thousands on the trains from Liverpool Street. The huge framework of the Zeppelin gleamed in the sunshine, reminding him of the skeleton of a prehistoric reptile. Stallholders, selling minerals and refreshments, were already thriving, as were farmworkers selling tiny pieces of metal or fabric as souvenirs. The blackened bodies of the Germans were a frightful spectacle in a nearby barn. The airship commander had jumped from his gondola, and the impression of his spreadeagled body, several inches deep in the soil, remained as a curiosity.

The bombs of the Zeppelins left more scars across the city; Macdonagh saw "ugly gaps and gashes, exposed blackened rooms, wallpaper hanging in tatters, pictures awry, stairs ending in mid-air, furniture broken and covered with a thick dust of lath and plaster." Enterprising children dug shrapnel fragments from the wood-block road surface to sell as souvenirs, while others were seen parading the streets singing "Keep the Homes Fires Burning." In a slum district, Sylvia Pankhurst noticed a wrecked chapel where the broken wall displayed the text, "A new commandment I give unto you: that ye love one another." Wreaths of artificial flowers stood on the windowsills of damaged houses for the victims within; beside them pathetic cardboard box lids were placed to collect pennies for the freshly orphaned children or to replace shattered furniture.

On October 1st, a decisive blow was struck at the Zeppelin venture, when the famous Commander Mathy died as his ship crashed in flames at Potters Bar. His death marked the end of the Zeppelin as a useful weapon.

However, on 28th November, 1916, while Britain celebrated the destruction of two more Zeppelins, air-raids took a new turn. A single aeroplane ventured to fly to London and dropped six bombs. It was the first aeroplane attack on the city. *The Times* rightly saw the raid as an ominous sign: "We have always believed that the method of raiding by aeroplanes, which are relatively cheap and elusive, has far more dangerous possibilities than the large and costly Zeppelin." The editor of the *Nation* believed that aerial bombing was only just beginning, that "in the next few years, science will have invented airships capable of carrying tons of such high explosive, that a single bomb dropped in the centre of a largish town will utterly destroy the whole of it . . . Rome, Venice, Canterbury and Oxford will become as Ypres and the inhabitants of every city dwell in perpetual dread." The Gotha bombers of 1917, which brought new terror to air-raids, showed that the war in the air had begun in earnest.

Opposite. The blazing wreck of a Zeppelin, which fell at Cuffley, September 1916.

4 *1917*

"... And the wind
Blowing over London from Flanders
Has a bitter taste."
    Richard Aldington, "Sunsets"

State Control

LLOYD GEORGE, who became Prime Minister in December, 1916, brought a new sort of Government to rule the war effort. He and a small five-man war cabinet were the decision makers. Under them were the old Departments of State, now joined by new ministries (shipping, food, labour, food production and National Service). They were housed in converted London hotels or clubs and employed large numbers of clerks, mostly women. As their influence began to reach into all corners of national life, people became used to filling in a great variety of forms. The new regime was nearly a dictatorship. The Government, giving itself extended powers under D.O.R.A., could seize land or factories and houses, buy up whole stocks of goods (thus all 1916 wool production, leather and hay crop were taken for the Army), refuse to allow men to work at non-essential trades (like house painting, printing or hotel waiting), control railways and shipping (petrol for private motoring almost vanished in 1917). There was some protest against this new kind of government. *The Times* complained about the "gigantic and apparently unchecked growth of ministerial establishments." They were expensive and clumsy, and there were clashes between ministries about who controlled particular activities. The general effect of this new government was a movement towards state control, what some called "collectivism" and others "war socialism."

The individual was now bound by the extra complications of D.O.R.A. Here are some of the things that the tangle of regulations forbade him to do by 1917:
1. Talk about naval or military matters in public places.
2. Spread rumours about military affairs.
3. Trespass on railways or bridges.
4. Use code when writing abroad.
5. Light bonfires or fireworks.
6. Fly kites.
7. Buy binoculars.
8. Melt down gold or silver.
9. Give bread to any dog, poultry or horse.
10. Trespass on allotments.
11. Say anything offensive about British or Allied Armies.
There were many other points in the web of rules. The police, given new, extraordinary powers in wartime, could arrest any suspect, or could enter any premises at any time. The public helped as unofficial spies.

Opposite. David Lloyd George, who became Prime Minister in December 1916. From *Punch*, captioned "The New Conductor: opening of the 1917 overture."

Below. In 1917 Government departments obtained increasing control of the daily lives of British people. D.O.R.A. is the powerful Defence of the Realm Act, a vast web of war regulations. Cartoon from *London Opinion*, by Wilton Williams, captioned "The Official (to D.O.R.A.): 'Go and see what the British Public is doing – and tell it not to.'"

The women's services: Wrens acting as messengers to ships and a poster for the Women's Royal Air Force (their uniform was considered the smartest).

The story of D. H. Lawrence and his German wife is an interesting illustration. Unfit for war, he lived in a Cornish cottage. Neighbours heard the Lawrences singing German songs and they were accused of signalling to German submarines. Lawrence's cottage was ransacked and his notebooks confiscated. He was expelled from Cornwall and ordered to report regularly to the police. His novel *The Rainbow* had already been banned in 1916 because of its unfavourable comments about soldiers. The public accepted their new restricted lives, but found it strange to look back on old 1914 freedoms.

Women at War

By 1917, Britain was a country of women, children and old men; another, ever-changing population in khaki came and went. The women's war effort reached a new peak in this year. The female industrial workers showed off their new affluence. Macdonagh watched girls at the fair on Hampstead Heath at Whitsun: "They had laid aside their furs and velveteens and high-laced boots, and turned out in the summer finery of coloured sports-coats, white and pink dresses and low shoes." Sales of jewellery, silk-stockings, fur coats and the status symbol, the piano, were rising rapidly. Women's ready-made dress shops enjoyed success (in contrast to men's tailors, as so many young officers died before their uniform bills were paid).

New uniforms were seen in the streets as women joined the armed services to take up non-combatant duties to free men for battle: about 100,000 girls served as auxiliaries up to 1918. Most joined the Women's Auxiliary Army Corps (W.A.A.C.), which was formed in 1917 from the 1914 Women's Legion of cooks and drivers. There was the Women's

"Our Amazon Corps Standing Easy." A *Punch* cartoon makes fun of the W.A.A.C.S. In fact, their life, when in France was often harsh and dangerous.

Formidable-looking women police.

One of the thousands of
V.A.D. nurses.

Royal Air Force (W.R.A.F.) and Women's Royal Naval Service (W.R.N.S.). They all wore uniforms in appropriate colours – that of the W.R.A.F.'s was considered "decidedly ornamental," and even the shapeless tunics and skirts could not prevent "sex from breaking through in bright eyes, shapely ankles and ripe, red lips." All were officered by "ladies of breeding and education." The duties of the W.R.N.S. in decoding operations were perhaps the most important of their varied tasks; the women's service also supplied drivers, clerks, cooks, storekeepers, typists and even gardeners in military cemeteries. Although there were rumours about the immorality of "Les Tommettes" in France, sternly denied by authority, their service life was often drab in rough quarters, and dangerous where they came under enemy air bombardment. Following their gallantry during the 1918 German March Offensive, the W.A.A.C.'s became Queen Mary's Army Auxiliary Corps.

Women Police were another new service, "true friends of the girls" needed in a world of working girls. Their success in London in dealing with theft, disorder and drunkenness led most cities to employ them, and their severe dark blue uniforms and hard felt hats became familiar in the streets. The *Evening News* described their power: "In many cases, the policewoman does not even have to speak. She just looks and he who is looked at melts thoughtfully away."

The most arduous of war work was done by the thousands of V.A.D.'s (Voluntary Aid Detachment), who assisted as nurses or orderlies in hospitals at home and in all the major theatres of war. Many middle and upper class girls, brought up in a world of sheltered security, endured the severe fatigue of hospital routine. "I was nineteen, very carefully brought up and severely chaperoned," one V.A.D. told Mrs. Peel. "I passed suddenly to being a little person who spent her time in a hospital, freeing from lice the uniforms of the soldiers who were brought in." They were faced with the horrible suffering caused by battle wounds. "When I undressed my clothes reeked of pus," wrote one girl, while another recalled the gas victims: "The burned and sightless eyes made all the faces look like a ghastly row of masks." In her moving book *Diary without Dates* (1918), Enid Bagnold, a wartime V.A.D., described a hospital next to an Army camp: "From the camp across the roads the words of command float in through the ward window. 'Halt!' and 'Left wheel!' and 'Right wheel!' . . . All day long the words of command come over the ward window-sills. All day they bump and shout and sweat . . . All day long little men training to fill just such another hospital as ours with other little men . . ."

The "flapper," with her bobbed hair and short skirt, engaged in a restless hunt for pleasure, was another kind of wartime girl. Chaperones, who had accompanied the upper-class girl to dances before the war, now disappeared: there was new freedom. Life seemed short and was to be enjoyed; the need to relax from mental strain, or war work, or to forget recent horrors led to more smoking, drinking and drug taking among these girls. 1917 saw the growth of the dancing mania. In the many nightclubs that had sprung up in London's West End, jazz bands played the latest "ragtime" tunes like the gay but poignant "Everybody's doin' it, doin' it, doin' it." A girl, recalling the dancing craze for Mrs. Peel, wrote: "Looking back on the war years, we seem to have been very callous . . . Although most of us did some kind of war-work, we used to dance almost every night. Sometimes at these dances, there was a small band, often only a piano . . . The men looked so nice in uniform . . . Life was very gay. It was only when someone you knew well or with whom you were in love was killed that you minded really dreadfully. Men used to come to dine and dance one night, and go out the next morning and be killed. And someone used to say, 'Did you see poor Bobbie was killed?' It went on all the time, you see."

The "flappers" seemed to the newspapers to symbolize the immorality of wartime "with their high heels, skirts up to their knees and blouses open to the diaphragm, painted, powdered, self-consciously ogling." Constant fear of death produced a rash of hasty marriages, which were often tragically brief, a mere honeymoon in a few days' leave. Young wives were all too soon young widows.

Passchendaele : Mud, Casualties and Doubts

The Western Front fighting in 1917 was dominated by the British Army. Sir Douglas Haig (1861–1928), the British Commander-in-Chief, launched a major offensive on 31st July, striking from Ypres towards the

The nightmare battle in the mud: Third Ypres, 1917.

Belgian coast. There had been much doubtful questioning by the British War Cabinet, who had only been finally won over by the promise that U-boat harbours would be captured in Belgium. Exceptionally wet weather turned the ground, churned up by the millions of shells fired in bombardment of German positions, into a sea of mud. The delicate drainage system of the flat Flanders plain was destroyed and men literally drowned in the swamps. The advance became a nightmare. A four mile advance to the Passchendaele ridge took four months and cost 324,000 casualties. The landscapes of third Ypres were like something from Dante's "Inferno". They were described in the powerful poems of Siegfried Sassoon, which caused much interest in Britain. In contrast to the romantic visions of the 1915 "war poets," Sassoon created war scenes of ugly realism.

> "The place was rotten with dead; green clumsy legs
> High-booted, sprawled and grovelled along the saps;
> And trunks, face downward, in the sucking mud,
> Wallowed like trodden sand-bags loosely filled;
> And naked sodden buttocks, mass of hair,
> Bulged, clotted heads slept in the plastering slime
> And then the rain began . . . ."

Only at Cambrai, in November, was there any real success. Here a breakthrough by massed tanks brought a temporary victory that was

Blinded victims of the fighting in France.

celebrated in Britain by the ringing of church bells, which had been silenced since 1914.

The horror of the Western Front was reflected in the numbers of wounded seen in the streets. At Brighton, Caroline Playne, saw "hundreds of men on crutches going about in groups, many having lost one leg, many others both legs . . . The maiming of masses of strong, young men thus brought home was appalling." This spectacle seemed to give little surprise to passers-by; people were becoming used to the cruelty and waste of the war. There were also the gassed, with their dreadful deep coughs, or the blind, whose fate brought this pitiful advertisement in *The Times*: "Lady, fiancé killed, will gladly marry officer totally blinded or otherwise incapacitated by the war." Sassoon, himself a "shell shock" victim, wrote movingly in *Sherston's Progress* of those wounded in the mind, in a mental hospital in Edinburgh: "By night they lost control and the hospital became sepulchral and oppressive . . . One lay awake and listened to feet padding along passages which smelt of stale cigarette smoke . . . One became conscious that the place was full of men whose slumbers were morbid and terrifying – men muttering uneasily or suddenly crying out in their sleep. Around me was that underworld of dreams haunted by submerged memories of warfare and its intolerable shocks . . ."

The "Fight to the Finish" mentality still dominated public opinion. A few lone voices were ignored. The Society of Friends, in a message to the world, asked: "How long are the peoples to go on killing one another? . . . Are we not multiplying evil and planting the seeds of bitterness which can never bear the fruit of peace?" H. G. Wells, who had welcomed the "war to end war" in 1914, now wrote sombrely in the *Daily News*: "Why does the waste and killing go on? . . . [statesmen] chaffer like happy imbeciles while civilization bleeds to death." A letter to the *Daily Telegraph* from Lord Lansdowne, the former Foreign Secretary, suggesting an immediate compromise peace, attracted widespread anger as "a stab in the back" or "a white flag." The insatiable war machine ran on. "Whole battalions of fathers, husbands, brothers enter the inferno and melt away like summer snow," wrote Caroline Playne. "Our streets are filled with the halt and the blind, and a load of sorrow is accumulating in every home in the land."

Gothas and Giants

After the fiery doom of the Zeppelins, a mood of confidence about air-raids swept across Britain. In London, the lights were brightened, guns moved away, pilots and aircraft returned to France. But their first defeat only stimulated the Germans to attack with a superior weapon, the bombing aeroplane, first the twin-engined Gothas, then the huge four-engined Giant machines. In the spring, they attacked the Kent coast in the first of many air raids. "Bright silver insects" appeared over Folkestone, their bombs leaving 95 dead and 290 injured. The grim, mass burials were, in the Archbishop of Canterbury's words, the "honourable price of being the bit of England nearest the enemy." Soon citizens of Dover were hastening to the caves cut in the chalk cliffs to

Opposite. A little girl stares at some of the hundreds of wounded and crippled to be seen in Brighton.

shelter from the frequent attacks.

At midday, on 13th June, 1917, the Gothas came in massed formation to attack London, the white aircraft standing out against a blue summer sky. People thought they were British machines on exercise and stopped to watch. "The sight was so magnificent that I stood spellbound," remembered Mrs. Peel. A woman on a bus, interviewed by Mrs. Peel, recalled how curiosity was the first reaction of London crowds: "The conductor was hanging onto the stairway rail and bending backwards, staring into the sky . . .all the people on the pavement were staring, too . . . the omnibus stopped and the conductor said 'You'd best take cover.'" Liverpool Street Station was the main target. Seventy-two bombs showered onto the area. Amid the crashes of the bombs, shattering of glass and slates, and terrified screams, fire-engines and khaki military ambulances swerved through the traffic. Vera Brittain, the nurse, remembered the shrapnel "raining down like a thunder shower" on the trees in Kensington Gardens; then, going into the City, she found the streets "terrifyingly quiet" and "so thickly covered with broken glass that I seemed to be wading ankle-deep in huge unmelted hailstones." The only signs of violence were "a crimson-splashed horse lying indifferently on its side, and several derelict tradesmen's carts bloodily denuded of their drivers."

Basements of offices and shops were packed during the raid. In one of these – at a school in Poplar – came the most tragic incident. A large bomb pierced three floors and exploded in a cellar where sixty infants were sheltering. Sixteen were killed and thirty badly injured. A soldier

Above. The London underground railway provided a refuge from the bombs.
Walter Baye's painting *The Underworld.*

Left. N. Arnold's painting *Daylight Air-Raid* shows German Gotha bombers over
London.

on leave was first into the building and saw the room "choked with
struggling and screaming victims, many of them crying distractedly for
their mothers. Little limbs were blown from bodies, and unrecognizable
remains were littered among the debris of broken desks and forms." The
funeral of the dead children was marked by real grief. "One saw people
sobbing in an hysterical, heartbroken way," noted Caroline Playne.
"Such unrestrained displays of grief in public in England are rare and
denote shock as well as grief." A wreath was marked, "To our children
murdered by German aircraft." The raid's complete toll, – 162 killed
and 432 injured – was the heaviest of the war.

On 7th July, the Gothas returned. This time they seemed "huge,
sharply defined, mobile magazines of death" against a grey sky, like "a
collection of cholera germs on a glass disc." The bombers kept careful
V-formation as they circled the dome of St. Paul's Cathedral. Then they
dropped their bombs and fifty more Londoners died. A near hysterical
wave of anger broke in the press. After her "victories" on land and sea,
Britain was dishonoured by this defeat in the air. *John Bull* magazine
demanded revenge under the heading, "Six bombs for one." "Hit back
and hit hard! . . . I say that the Huns, vicious in victory, cowards in
defeat, deserve no more consideration than a mad dog or a venomous
snake – and that it is our duty to the humanity they have outraged . . .
to carry death and devastation into the heart of their country as they have
spread death and destruction throughout Europe. To Hell with pacifists,
praters, Party politicians . . . The lives of our citizens and the honour of
our country are at stake. We're out for War – let it be War to the Death!"

A fresh outburst of anti-German rioting swept through the hard hit East End. Eventually, under a new Air Minister, efforts were made to deliver reprisals, and plans were made for a Royal Air Force bombing squadron. Several large bombers were ready to fly to attack Berlin by November 1918.

General Smuts, the old Boer Leader, now in the British High Command, was placed in charge of London's defences. The City was ringed with artillery. Mobile guns on lorries moved to follow the raiders. First-rate fighter squadrons were recalled from France and experimental barrage balloons, trailing curtains of steel streamers, were sent aloft. On coasts early warning listening-posts, large ear trumpets – manned sometimes by blind men – caught the first throbs of the Gotha engines. An elaborate warning system was devised. Policeman in cars or on bicycles carried "Take Cover" notices through the streets, lights flashed on and off, and exploding sound rockets, "maroons," were fired from police stations. Blue-lighted signs guided people to shelters in substantial buildings. Co-ordinated ambulances and fire-engines, demolition squads of engineers, and hospitals stood ready.

The precautions were most necessary. In September, the Germans launched a sequence of day and night raids, the forerunner of the "Blitz" of the 1940's. In a single attack, 276 incendiaries fell on the city. This time the Gothas were supplemented by the clumsy Giant bombers. These raids caused widespread panic, which the Government tried to calm by telling the Press to give less coverage, especially in their photographs, to damage and casualties. People in London began to look pale and nerve-wracked. While large dugouts were planned for them in the Royal Parks, Londoners sought safety elsewhere. Houses and rooms were keenly sought in the safe south-west suburbs like Richmond and Kingston. Others flocked to the Thames tunnels. Most popular of all were the Underground stations, where people crowded to pass uncomfortable nights squeezed onto platforms and stairs, even in lifts. When the maroons went off, "the pattering of feet began." Mrs. Peel

Air-raid victims in London.

Opposite. Tragic child victims in a London school, hit by bombs from the first daylight air-raid, June 1917. From the *Sphere*.

93

The call for reprisals was not effective until British bombers were ready in autumn 1918. Cartoon from *Punch*.
Caption reads:
"*Prime Minister*. 'You young rascal! I never said that.'"
"*Newsboy*. 'Well, I'll lay yer meant it.'"

saw hundreds of people who "hurried along the darkened streets carrying children and pillows and shawls and food. One heard only the noise of these many quickly moving feet and the occasional stumble of some sleepy child."

The blackout was now almost completely effective. Even trains masked their fires and switched off their lights during an alert. Above the city, Cecil Lewis, an R.F.C. pilot, saw only aerodrome flares and searchlights. "London itself was a dark crouching monster within . . . Here and there a tiny pin-point of light marked the existence of human beings upon an earth which seemed otherwise reserved to trees and waters and the moon," he observed in *Sagittarius Rising*. The bomber pilots, unlike those of the Zeppelins, preferred moonlit nights when they could easily follow the Thames. Under the harvest moon of the autumn of 1917, London fearfully awaited the enemy: "Strangely quiet and deserted were the streets," wrote Cecil Lewis, . . . street lights were no more than glowing pin-points along the shadowy chasms between the houses . . . pedestrians hurried by quickly in the shadow of walls, glancing apprehensively at the sky. Would they come tonight? London seemed breathless, in the tense expectancy of disaster." Walking home at night, Michael Macdonagh saw an apparently empty city: "The only sound was that of my own solitary footfalls in the ghostly moonlight. Yet I surmised that [the] occupants, far from being asleep, were very wide awake and alert . . . I could see at any upper window, now and then, a curtain drawn a little aside, and a face peering out cautiously as if to see whether the appearance of some human being in the road signified that the overhanging terror had passed away."

After the danger was gone, Macdonagh recalled a different mood of relief. "What is that sound afar off and faint? A bugle surely? Nearer and nearer it comes. Yes, it is the 'All Clear!' Hurrah! And like all our neighbours, we rush out into the road, and cheer and clap our hands as the Boy Scout on a bicycle dashes past blowing the joyful tidings on his bugle."

The air-raids continued until May, 1918. In all there were twenty aeroplane attacks on the capital, causing 836 deaths and wounding 1,982. The huge moral effect of the bombers was out of all proportion to the relatively slight damage and tiny air fleets which were involved.

Children and the War

> What can a little chap do
> For his country and for you?

So began a popular poem about a child's wartime duty. He was expected to "do his bit" with the adults. There was collecting for the war effort: silver paper, wool, rags, even horse chestnuts, supposedly useful for munitions. He could help with War Savings schemes, and many schools ran jumble sales, and concerts for this purpose. He could buy cigarettes and sweets to take on visits to wounded soldiers. Girls, of course, knitted and sewed. Both sexes helped with farm work or on allotments. Boy Scouts and Girl Guides did work of real value, especially as messengers, stretcher-bearers, or as signallers in air-raids.

Opposite. "Have they gone?" Frightened crowds shelter from the German daylight aeroplane raiders, July 1917. From the *Sphere*.

94

Children were subjected to the same propaganda that drenched society. Sir James Yoxall, M.P. kindly explained the war to young people in *Why Britain went to War* (1916). "In all this war there is nothing for us to be ashamed of: We fight for honour. You know what honour is among schoolboys – straight dealing, truth speaking, and 'playing the game.' Well, we are standing up for honour among nations, while Germany is playing the sneak and the bully in the big European school. Germany must be taught to 'play cricket,' to play fair, to honour 'a scrap of paper.' A boy who behaved as Germany has done would be 'sent to Coventry' by all the School."

In school, the local Roll of Honour was read, while the children turned to salute the flag. Boys proudly wore metal copies of their fathers' regimental badges; some even had miniature uniforms. "Victories" were celebrated (some luckless babies were even named after battles: "Verdun," for example, was a popular name for girls, as was "Mons" for boys). Special days were set aside to study Allied countries. Thus on "Russian Day," the history, geography and literature of that country would be briefly introduced, as "it is our duty to know the good side of the Russians." Children sang national and patriotic songs:

Above. A Boy Scout sounds the "All Clear" after a night raid. Boy Scouts made a valuable war contribution by acting as messengers.

Opposite. A child dressed in miniature uniform stands proudly by his father.

> "There's a land, a dear land,
> Where the rights of the free
> Are as firm as the earth
> And as wide as the sea.
> Where the primroses bloom
> And the nightingales sing
> And an honest poor man
> Is as good as the King.
> Home of brave men and the girls they adore,
> Westland, best land, my land, thy land,
> England wave-guarded and green to the shore,
> God bless our Empire and King evermore."

The children also had their own kind of patriotic song:

> "At the cross, at the cross,
> Where the Kaiser lost his hoss
> And the eagle on his hat flew away;
> They were eating currant buns
> When they heard the British guns
> And the frightened little beggars ran away."

Schooling suffered considerably in many areas. Schools were taken over by the Army or turned into hospitals, and children squeezed into churches or public halls, sometimes on a double shift system giving half-time education. Conscription took men teachers to the Army, leaving women to manage alone. The Board of Education tried to make the best of things, commenting favourably in its 1914–15 Report on new school activities: "The half day out of school has sometimes been used to excellent purposes for games and physical exercise, swimming, open air work, excursions, visits to museums and galleries, needlework parties and the like . . ."

Not surprisingly, there was an increase in juvenile delinquency. A

F

1917 Report noted an increase of between 30 and 50 per cent. in charges against young people in seventeen of Britain's largest cities. Theft and gambling were most common offences. The factors considered to cause this sudden rise in crime are interesting in throwing light on working class life in the war. Not only fathers and elder brothers, now in the Army, were missing from home, but perhaps the mothers, too, were in war industry. To economize, there was more house-sharing among families, leading to overcrowding. Another cause was blackout which provided cover for theft. Films could be blamed too: "They make children, whose thoughts should be happy and wholesome, familiar with ideas of death by exhibiting shootings, stabbings and the like." A social worker, Cecil Leeson, commented, in his book *The Child and the War* (1917) on the prevailing moods of violence and adventure and their effect on a boy. "He is plastic, impressionable, imitative, a mirror to every breath of national feeling . . . today is the day of the hero – and a boy dearly wishes to be thought a hero. He, too, desires adventures, and no doubt an innocent wagon creeping stealthily through a dark, mean street does sometimes prove to be 'a German Convoy' . . . Moreover, the prevailing war-talk, compounded as it largely is of craft, guile, revenge, does not serve to improve matters . . ."

On the other hand, the child also gained from the war. Despite the food shortages, Board of Education Medical Reports of the war years noted that children were healthier and better clothed, results of war work prosperity in the family. Older boys and girls could earn substantial wages. In 1917, the authorities calculated that at least 600,000 children had gone prematurely to work, evading the loosely upheld leaving age of fourteen. A 1917 Report on Juvenile Education deplored this, seeing "deterioration in behaviour and morality. Gambling has increased. Excessive hours of strenuous labour have overtaxed the powers of young people, while many have taken advantage of the extraordinary demand for juvenile labour to change even more rapidly than usual from one blind alley employment to another."

Plainly urgent action was necessary. Lloyd George appointed H. A. L. Fisher, Vice Chancellor of Sheffield University, to draw up educational reforms. The new Educational Act was passed in mid-1918. "It is framed to repair the intellectual wastage which has been caused by the war," said Fisher. It also aimed to limit "the industrial pressure upon the

child life of this country." The provision of secondary education begun in 1902 was extended. The leaving age was to be fourteen, with ambitious "day continuation" classes giving further part-time education up to eighteen. All fees were abolished. The Burnham Committee was set up to give teachers better salaries and proper pensions. There was to be more medical care and better nursery schools. The Act was greeted with enthusiasm by *The Times* in a leading article: "A real guarantee will have been given to the working classes that their sons and daughters will find the doors of life opening to their knock. Such a guarantee gives them the fair share of the freedom and justice which we tell them we are fighting to maintain; it gives a concrete value and meaning to an abstract ideal." Sadly most of the reforms were never carried out. Impoverished by the war, Britain was unable to provide schools fit for heroes' children.

Blockade and Shortages

"There can now be heard the footsteps of a power indifferent even to righteous causes," wrote Caroline Playne of 1917. Famine was the spectre that haunted Britain and Germany as their mutual sea blockades tightened. Britain had long ceased to be self-sufficient: heavy quantities of food for her forty-five million inhabitants were imported. In early February, the Germans declared unrestricted submarine war on Britain. All ships sailing to and from British ports were to be sunk at sight by the new long-range U-boats. During the last four months of 1916, 532,000 tons of British shipping had been sunk; in the single month of April 1917, 526,000 tons went to the bottom. Industry was simply unable to replace the losses. A Food Economy poster declared gloomily, "It takes four months to build a ship, and four minutes to sink one." At the end of April, Britain had wheat stores to last only six weeks. The President of the Board of Trade feared "a complete breakdown in shipping would come before June 1917." The solution, forced through the Admiralty by Lloyd George himself, was the convoy system, whereby merchant ships sailed in groups protected by destroyer escorts. Nonetheless, 1917 was a grim year in Britain, with sharply rising prices, shortages and queues.

Lloyd George had already responded to the threat of shortage by creating a Ministry of Food in December, 1916. The first Food Con-

An advertisement produced by Michelin, the French tyre company, showing the intrepid Michelin man reaching England from France, despite attacks from Zeppelins and submarines. Unrestricted submarine warfare on England was declared in February 1917.

troller, Lord Devonport, and his network of local food Committees, operated a voluntary economy campaign, mostly ineffective. The voluntary ration scheme (four pounds of bread, two and a half pounds of meat, three quarters of a pound of sugar each week) was out of touch with social reality. Most working men still lived chiefly on bread. The propagandists sent round to lecture on eating less, addressed crowds of people "who had never had enough to eat, who, indeed, had never had enough of anything except privation and of that too much." They modified their message to "use as little as you can." Although the King and Queen dutifully limited themselves to the voluntary ration (a badge of purple ribbon was issued to people who followed the royal example), the wealthy still seemed to have plenty to eat. You could dine luxuriously at

England's dread enemy—not Wilhelm, but Waste

An ounce of food saved now is worth a pound at harvest time

England's enemies, Huns, hoarders, and heedless housewives

Save your Food, Save your Country!

the Ritz, and, at the traditional Lord Mayor's Banquet in London, Macdonagh noticed "such was the demand for roast beef that the carvers were kept very busy cutting the huge barons into slices." In ordinary restaurants, meatless and potato-less days were ordered. Food producing and food saving exhibitions were sent round, and, in case of extreme shortage, a National Kitchen scheme was prepared to provide minimal food cooked at public centres. The food rules were extremely complicated and often aimed at trivialities. For instance, it was forbidden to sell crumpets, throw rice at weddings, use sugar icing, feed scraps to animals or birds, or stiffen collars with starch. Nor were efforts to control prices successful: the controlled items at once disappeared from the shops.

There were certain particular shortages. The potato harvest had been poor in 1916. Crowds besieged farmers selling seed potatoes at markets. Experts came forward to explain that one-fifth of the food value was contained in the skin, which should therefore be eaten. Sugar, two-thirds of which had been refined from German beet before the war, was extremely scarce, and was to be the first food to be rationed. No longer did it appear on café tables. The waitress brought it round. Jam making was especially hard-hit and tons of fruit were wasted. A drive was made to economize on bread, as wheat was so desperately short. There were new slogans on the posters: "Eat less bread and victory is secure." An official handout said, "Look well at the loaf on your breakfast table and treat it as if it were real gold because that British loaf is going to beat the German . . . Today the kitchen is the key to victory and is in the fighting line alongside our undying heroes of the trenches . . ." Another Ministry leaflet had a crust speaking for itself:"

"I am a slice of Bread . . .
I am wasted once a day by 48,000,000 people of Britain.
I am 'the bit left over'; the slice eaten absent mindedly
When really I wasn't needed: I am the waste crust.

Food queues became longer everywhere as the submarine campaign cut off Britain's food supplies.

If you collected me and my companions for a whole week you would find that we amounted to 9380 tons of good bread – WASTED! Nine shiploads of good bread!...
SAVE ME, AND I WILL SAVE YOU!"

Substitute breads, made of potato or bean flour, began to appear. Butter and margarine were in short supply. Frightening photographs in the Press in December showed rows of empty hooks in the meat market at Smithfield.

Shortage caused queues outside shops, sometimes containing thousands of people. Mrs. Peel watched them: "In the bitter cold and rain of that depressing winter . . ., women and children waited outside the shabby shops common to the poor districts of all towns. They carried baskets, string-bags, fish-boxes, bags made of American cloth, and babies, and stood, shifting their burdens from one arm to another to ease their aching arms." *The Times* reported the growing phenomenon in London: "Outside the dairy shops of certain multiple firms in some parts of London, women began to line up for margarine as early as five o'clock on Saturday morning . . . over a thousand people waited for margarine at a shop in New Broad Street . . . and in Walworth Road . . . the queue was estimated to number about three thousand . . ." People did not only queue for food – fuel was equally short. At railway coal-sidings waited pathetic lines of people with prams, wheel-barrows, sacks, boxes or baskets. In October, coal was rationed, according to the number of rooms in the house. Those with nothing else to burn collected scraps of wood, or beachcombed for rubbish along rivers or shores.

One remedy for shortages was home-grown food on the allotment. Gardens, tennis courts, parks, school-fields, odd scraps of waste land beside railways were cultivated for vegetables. By May, there were said to be half a million allotments, following the slogan "Idle land for Food." England had never looked so green as in the summer of 1917. Severe penalties were imposed on thieves, and patrols kept jealous watch. Again authority led the way. The King, even the Queen – who wrote in her diary "worked from 3 to 5 planting potatoes. Got very hot and tired" – dug their Buckingham Palace plot, and Lloyd George grew King Edward potatoes in his garden. Not only was the extra food production substantial, the creative work of cultivation was also good therapy: "Many a sorrow was buried in these war gardens," wrote Mrs. Peel, "and many a man and woman learned the joy of tilling the earth."

While city men hurried home to dress up as farm labourers to cultivate new ground, the drain of farm workers into the Army in 1914 meant that good farm land had fallen into disuse. The pre-war agricultural decline and the spread of towns gave only eleven million acres of farm land in 1914. Lloyd George told the new Board of Agriculture that "Britain must be put in the way to feed herself." The Board lived up to its telegram address "GROWMORE." It had powers under D.O.R.A. to take over land, remove inefficient farmers or take over stocks of seed or fertilizers. By 1918 an extra three million acres had come under the plough. All kinds of new labour was used: soldiers, prisoners of war, conscientious objectors, teams of children. The Women's Land Army, most attractive of all the women's work schemes, contributed enormously.

" 'Keep the Home Fires Burning.' Solo by our optimistic Premier." So runs the caption to this *Punch* cartoon. But Lloyd George's dynamic leadership sustained Britain in the dark war years, 1917–18.

The Women's Land Army helped to revive Britain's decayed agriculture in 1917–18.

Right. Allotments to help food supplies became a national craze in 1917. From *Punch.*

Below. Eton schoolboys prepare to "do their bit" on the College allotments.

260,000 girls were employed by 1918. At local agricultural shows, farmers were astonished to see girls ploughing perfect furrows or handling threshing machines or spreading manure. In London, Macdonagh watched a Land Army recruiting rally in Hyde Park: "There were in the procession two hay-wagons, each drawn by a pair of fine farm-horses and driven by girls. The wains were decorated with sheaves of corn, branches of yew, box and broom, and daffodils, telling of the charms of spring and autumn on the land, and emphasizing the invitation of one of the banners, 'Come with us into the country' and in each was a choir of girls, singing land songs, including even 'The Farmer's Boy' . . . Most picturesque and captivating of all were the girls themselves. They all wore smocks, knicker-bockers, high-legged boots and felt hats . . . How well nourished and blooming the girls looked! What a contrast to the pale and painted girls among the spectators!"

The New Hope

In the austere Britain of 1917, the entry of America into the war in April brought new hope and purpose. The idealism of President Wilson (1856–1924) set out eventually as the Fourteen Points, his basis for a lasting peace settlement, gave new shape to Britain's confused war aims (it had always been odd for "democratic" Britain to fight on the side of autocratic Russia, for example). According to the journalist, Hall Caine, the declaration marked the "National Marriage" of Britain and America: "In the name of justice, of mercy, of religion, of human dignity, of all that makes man's life worth living, and distinguishes it from the life of the Brute, America has drawn the sword and thrown away the scabbard." The 20th April was declared as America Day. There was a special service at St. Paul's Cathedral; the sunlit streets were crowded with people wearing tiny American flags in their button holes, sold by street-hawkers; and over Parliament, the Union Jack and the Stars and Stripes floated side by side. When the first American soldiers marched through London in August, they seemed bigger and fresher than the weary soldiers of Europe, "fine fellows . . . tall, slim, athletic, with long, clean-shaven faces." The arrival of massed American soldiers was a portent of eventual victory for the Allies. In the bitter struggle, they were to have the greater strength.

By 1918 the war was a grim test of endurance. A message printed in *Punch* "To All at Home."

5 *1918*

"There was no forgiveness, no generous instinct, no large-hearted common-sense in any combatant nation of Europe. Like wolves they had their teeth in each other's throats, and would not let go, though all bloody and exhausted, until one should fall at the last gasp to be mangled by the others."

Philip Gibbs, *Realities of War*

Food Rationing

LLOYD GEORGE appreciated the vital importance of morale on the Home Front in sustaining the war effort. Adequate food was the basis of morale: "I realized the 'feeding of the multitude' was a matter of supreme importance." The work of the Ministry of Food in 1917 had done little to prevent shortages and cut food queues. New slogans, like "Eat slowly" or "Keep warm. You will need less food," did not help the half a million people dismally queuing in London during January and February. There was well founded resentment of wealthier people, who got more than their share by having food delivered or by sending servants to the shop backdoor. More ominously, swollen necks and other signs of malnutrition were becoming evident in the poorest people.

Although food supplies were now better (the harvest of 1917 had been a record one), the Government decided to introduce rationing. Lord Rhondda, the new Food Controller, began the ration scheme in London and the Home Counties, and gradually extended it to the rest of the country. Its main purpose was to provide fairer distribution of food (total consumption actually increased in 1918). Sugar was rationed in January. Then in April, forty million ration cards were issued for meat and bacon ("meat card") or butter, cheese and margarine ("food card"). Individuals registered with a local butcher or grocer could have fifteen ounces of meat, five ounces of bacon and four ounces of butter or margarine each week. It was a triumph of organization, the effects of which were immediate. Queues disappeared and did not return. "Not for months," said Macdonagh, "has the housewife done her shopping in circumstances so agreeable to her requirements and purse." Food seemed more fairly distributed too. Prime joints appeared in East End shops, while scraggy cuts were seen on shelves of West End butchers. In July, the first ration cards were withdrawn, and replaced by books of coupons for all rationed foods. Only tea, cheese and bread remained unrestricted. Prices remained high. In this way, the German food blockade was finally defeated.

Votes for Women

By 1918 it was calculated that one and a half million women had replaced men in all fields of work. Their huge contribution to the national effort wore away the strong, anti-feminist prejudices shown by pre-war

Opposite. Prayers before battle: a scene at St. Martin-in-the-Fields, near Charing Cross, London.

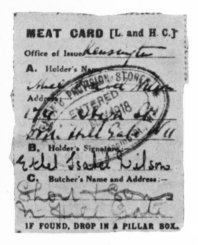

Above. Food rationing began in 1918. These are meat and fat cards.

Above right. Women clerks dealing with sugar cards, 1918. These women were just some of the thousands of clerks in the new wartime bureaucracies.

politicians. The bitterness aroused by the suffragette campaign of violence just before the war was now forgotten. One Liberal M.P. commented: "The women have made good their cause by their services where they had formerly spoilt it by their threats." Women's work in the munition factories seemed particularly impressive. Even Asquith, a strong opponent of the suffragettes, had become converted by 1916, when the House of Commons first approved the idea of votes for women.

The need to reform the franchise gave women this opportunity. A new Representation of the People Bill, part of the general 1918 promise of "reconstruction" for a better post-war world, made the vote almost universal for men (even soldiers under twenty-one). It also granted the vote to women over the age of thirty. This great women's victory was passed into law in June, 1918. One final stroke, in November, allowed women over twenty-one to stand as Members of Parliament.

Amid the stresses of the war, there was no great excitement about this democratic revolution, or about the six million new female voters. A great gathering of women war workers in Hyde Park in June celebrated women's new freedom. Macdonagh described the "wonderful sight. Girls in uniforms of many colours were to be seen. One group made a startling splash of scarlet. They wore vivid red robes that extended from head to feet. These were workers in factories where anti-gas masks are made. A large company of girls were dressed in creamy loose jackets and trousers, some with red caps and some with blue. There were V.A.D. nurses in blue dresses and white aprons; Post Office girls with their G.P.O. bags slung over their shoulders; girl bus conductors in their brown holland jackets; girl tram conductors in dark blue; girl foresters in brown jackets and bright green caps . . ." The size and variety of the parade was a tribute to women's war work. Now it was rewarded by that long sought token of the vote.

The German March Offensive

Having concluded peace with revolutionary Russia, Germany was free to bring more troops to France for a major offensive. On 21st March, they launched a formidable attack on the Western Front. The Allied Armies fell back in retreat. Throughout the spring, the German advance continued. They threatened Paris and even the vital Channel ports. All the ground so painfully won by the Allies in their great battles was again lost. The British Commander-in-Chief, Haig, issued his famous order: "With our backs to the wall and believing in the justice of our cause, each one of us must fight to the end."

In Britain it was a time of great bitterness. People in London looked pale, strained and anxious, yet Lloyd George noted "a grim resolve" on faces he met in the street. The battle could be clearly heard. Macdonagh, on Wimbledon Common, heard the artillery: "I soon became conscious of a curious atmospheric sensation, a kind of pulsation in regular beats . . . It was the guns – the terrible cannonade of the Great Battle in France which was shaking the earth literally and indeed the whole world metaphorically . . . The fearful thought took possession of me that this atmospheric shuddering, this subterranean tremor – was caused not so much by the guns as by the accompanying screams and groans of tens and thousands of mangled and terror-stricken men . . ."

Fresh casualties arrived at Charing Cross station. Mrs. Peel watched them: "The Khaki-clad girl chauffeurs drove away slowly so that they should not jolt wounded bodies. The flower women who sit with their baskets of blooms outside the station, threw their violets and roses, calling 'Cheerio!' and 'God bless you lads!' to the men who lay upon the stretchers." Fresh drafts were sent to the Front. There was little excitement about their departure. Macdonagh watched "a dark mass of men" march across Westminster Bridge. "They neither sang nor whistled. There was no 'Tipperary', no 'Goodbye, Piccadilly, goodbye, Leicester Square' . . . They marched on in silence save for the rhythmical tramp, tramp of their stout boots on the asphalt." He regretted this grim silence of the troops and agreed with *The Times* correspondent who asked for military bands for the troops. "Why should we not give the lads a real send-off, instead of smuggling them out of the country to which, perhaps some of them will never return?" A popular song of this time was intended to cheer the station partings; instead it came to share their melancholy:

"Good-bye – ee! Don't sigh – ee!
Wipe the tear, baby dear,
From your eye – ee.
Though it's hard to part I know,
I'll be tickled to death to go,
Don't sigh – ee! Don't cry – ee!
There's a silver lining in the sky – ee!
Bon soir, old thing! Cheerio, chin-chin!
Napoo! toodle-oo! Good-bye – ee!"

In Bristol, long convoys of lorries rumbled endlessly through the streets. Buildings vibrated as great caterpillar tractors pulled huge guns to the docks. These reinforcements stiffened British resistance, and the Allies held, then pushed back the German advance.

A fresh invasion scare set officials planning its repulse, with a militia or "home guard" of men up to sixty years old. This fear of imminent defeat brought more hysteria against aliens. An "intern them all" campaign began again, as Germans in Britain were said to be "crowing over" their armies' successes. A Hyde Park rally was arranged in August, after which a monster petition, carrying a million signatures on a two-mile roll of paper, was carried on a lorry decorated with Allied flags to 10, Downing Street. Thousands of ex-servicemen marched, under banners demanding "A clean sweep," singing patriotic songs. A letter to *The Times* caught the mood, condemning Germany as "a great heathen nation, hacking her way with deeds of devilish cruelty and with a never-ending stream of lies and tricks . . . To the people, the war is become a Holy War . . . of Heaven against Hell." German street names, of which there were many in Britain left from Prince Albert's time, were an easy target for local abuse. A Leicester local paper carried an angry letter: "Hun names must bring unpleasant memories to honourable people for generations to come . . . Is it fitting that our brave boys who have fought and bled should see such names when they return, or that those whose loved ones have gone west should be reminded of their murderers?" The popular film *Hearts of the World* recreated German atrocities in Belgium to impress audiences in a timely way. Cooler arguments, that many naturalized Germans had lost their sons who fought with the British Army, carried no weight. Conscientious objectors, too, were a target of intense hatred. They, like the German prisoners, were said to have too much food provided for them. By a cruel injustice, they were also deprived of their vote until several years after the war. Thus the anger and disappointment of the Home Front was directed at easy enemies in its midst.

Men and Money

The mighty counter-offensive that was launched in the summer of 1918, that was eventually to win the war, was costly in men and money. The Army was still short of soldiers, despite conscription and a "comb-out" of war industry in 1917. The popular newspapers launched a fresh campaign to "comb out the fit" from "overcrowded funk holes" in Government and industry. The munition workers were reviewed, and

In early 1918 the call-up was extended to men up to fifty years of age. Caption reads: "*Father*. 'Here's to the Fighter of Lucky Eighteen!' "*Son*. 'And here's to the Soldier of Fifty!' " (From *Punch*.)

104,000 of them released for the Army by June. Even the reluctant Miners' Unions allowed the release of 50,000 young men from the pits. Military Police rounded up men attending football, theatres, and music halls, making them produce evidence of exemption. The most desperate move came in April when a New Military Service Act raised the age of conscription to fifty-one. Middle-aged men, now to be soldiers, saw their businesses threatened with ruin. The journalist, G. S. Street, commented: "The call means in many cases the final touch of ruin to settled lives, with wives and children left to penury. They have grown grey in civilization and they are to be plunged into barbarism." However, none of the called-up men actually had to serve at the Front.

At the same time, fresh appeals were made for money. One the whole the Government relied on the vast wealth left from Victorian Britain to pay for the war. However, the war budgets increased income tax substantially, and imposed "super tax" on the wealthy. The Government also sold War Bonds and War Savings Certificates, offering the citizens generous 5 per cent. interest repayment for their money. "Lend your money to your country and keep the men at the Front" ran the slogan. New large-scale appeals were launched in 1917 and 1918. There was daily propaganda in the papers. "High and Low have been literally pouring out money in useless luxuries and amusement," said the writer of a propaganda leaflet. "The New War Loan gives us all a chance of making a fresh start and beginning here and now to do our duty by financing the war to the extent of every shilling that we can muster. The cause is surely big enough. Are we going to let this chance of helping it go by?"

Individual cities and towns could help by paying the cost of a particular weapon – a submarine, aircraft or war-ship. Tanks were displayed in town squares to attract funds to the "Tank Bank." These campaigns

A famous poster appeal by Frank Brangwyn. People began to hope for an end to the war during the autumn of 1918.

Mary Taylor, the actress, recites "Feed the Guns" at a campaign in Trafalgar Square, London.

were a huge success. If a town gave enough money, its name was painted on the tank's side to be carried proudly into battle. In London, the tank, with trench mud still on its sides, was introduced to the crowds by six girls, who had lost their sweethearts in the war. It is said to have gathered over £300,000 in a single week. In October, the equally popular "Feed the Guns" campaign saw a replica of a shell-shattered French village constructed in Trafalgar Square. Again the public was generous: throughout Britain "Feed the Guns" weeks raised £31 million.

About £600,000 million was collected by such voluntary subscriptions to help pay the enormous cost of the fighting (some £7 million a day by 1918). This was supplemented by taxation, by the sale of British investments overseas, and by loans from America. Unfortunately the money so obtained was often merely muddled away. Britain could afford the war, but the War Loan repayments and loss of trade markets were to remain as a drain on the national strength after the peace.

War Weariness

Daily life was increasingly wretched by 1918. In his *Memoirs*, Lloyd George recalled "The bewilderment and hardships of the time, war tiredness, the ghastly losses, the deepening and intensifying horrors of the struggle, the receding horizon of victory . . ." There was a hopeless feeling that the war would last for ever. The enforced pause of thousands of useful careers, the sorrow and hard work of women left behind produced an intense desire for peace. The world seemed "in conscienceless

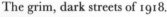
The grim, dark streets of 1918.

hands'' and the "power of darkness triumphant in every land."

Towns and cities now looked drab and shabby. By night London was gloomier, it was said, than it had been since the Middle Ages. Even by day the streets seemed sombre: people wore dark clothes, partly because of mourning, partly because of dye shortage. Shops stocked little but black and grey material. People, especially men, who dared to appear smartly dressed risked a jostling in the street for their lack of patriotic shabbiness.

Home life seemed in decline. The need for economies forced people to share houses or live in only a few rooms. The restless population movements, the absence of menfolk or the need to seek work, meant that many houses were shut up and furniture stored. Suburban avenues were lined with "To Let" boards. "These empty houses of suburbia," wrote Harold Owen, "each with its own separate story to tell of why it was empty and whither the inmates had gone, with their individual fates all merged into the great tragedy that engulfed the world. Broken homes, broken lives, broken hearts, far from the actual devastation of war . . ." The song, "Keep the Home Fires Burning" became increasingly un-realistic, as coal was rationed, and electricity and gas supplies reduced. People had to do without hot water. Ingenious cooking boxes, using hay, were devised to prepare meals, though more people sought ready-made meals at cheap restaurants. Any kind of war meeting became popular to fill the evenings or to allow an escape from cold, drab houses. Others simply went to bed earlier, while there was talk of a curfew for all citizens in the final winter of the war.

Travel was difficult and more expensive. Train fares rose by 50 per cent. in 1918, and services declined. In some districts, the very railway lines were pulled up to be sent to France. The petrol shortage reduced public transport like buses and taxis. The rush hour became, according to Mrs. Peel, "a daily terror. The crowds of office workers were vastly increased and the scramble to get into some of the longer distance trains and omnibuses constituted a bear fight out of which those of both sexes who were worsted or driven off the over-laden vehicles . . . retreated to the pavement with hats bashed in, umbrellas broken, shins and ankles kicked and bruised, in a dazed and shaken condition."

Holidays were considered unpatriotic. The seasonal Bank Holidays followed the sporting calendar into temporary oblivion. Foreign travel was not simply disapproved of but also dangerous in U-Boat infested seas. Tattered travel posters on stations reminded travellers of the happier pre-war world. "'Lovely Lucerne' was inaccessible," wrote Harold Owen. " 'Gay Boulogne' alas! was sad with military hospitals and busy with troops. Norwegian fiords and Swiss Alps still beckoned from the walls the traveller who could not go near them and as for the Rhine . . ."

Nor was it brighter outside the cities. A writer in the *Nation* described a visit to the West Country: "There, away from war's immediacy and stir, its secret and worst effects were revealed, the sea-waves giving up dead bodies from sunken ships, shores strewn with wreckage." With the shortage of timber from Norway, whole woods and forests were being felled, transforming and ruining the landscape. The great country

The rush hour became a "daily terror" in 1918 as transport services worsened.

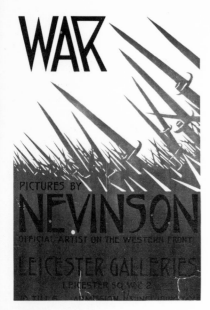

A poster for Nevinson's exhibition of war paintings.

houses, left from the nineteenth century, were now definitely dying, death duties and super tax combining to impoverish their owners. The poet Ezra Pound described the end of an age in his Canto LXXX:

"Is it all rust, ruin, death duties and mortgages,
And the great carriage-yard empty
And more pictures gone to pay taxes . . .?"

Despite the fresh wave of skilled war propaganda people looked at the war with more critical eyes. One observer noticed that the old jingoistic sentimental patriotism no longer pleased the audiences at music halls. This new realism was well represented in an artistic success of 1918, the Exhibitions of Paintings by the official war artists, sent by the Ministry of Information to record the war as they saw it. Paul Nash was the outstanding figure, widely praised in the Press. His theme was the landscape of the Western Front, with its broken trees and slime-filled shell holes. He wrote to his wife: "I am a messenger who will bring back word from the men who are fighting to those who want the war to go on for ever. Feeble, inarticulate, will be my message, but it will have a bitter truth, and may it burn their lousy souls."

In this atmosphere of fatigue and disillusion, strikes once more became a severe problem in industry. The strikes of April and May 1917 in vital war industries had lost one and a half million days' production. A government inquiry found various causes for malaise: the increasing inroads of conscription upon war industry workers, restrictions on the movement of labour, the use of unskilled workers, excessive overtime, grievances about wage rates, poor housing and expensive, inadequate food. There was resentment of profiteers. Moreover, there was the influence of communism from Russia. "The body corporate of the nation was assailed by a new infection," wrote Lloyd George in his *Memoirs*. "The coming of the Russian Revolution lit up the skies with a lurid flash of hope for all who were dissatisfied with the existing order of society."

The 1918 March offensive quietened the industrial unease for a time,

Strikes became a problem as war exhaustion grew in the autumn of 1918. From *London Opinion*.

as workers loyally supported the battle effort. From July onwards, there was increasing trouble, despite government protests that strikes were "as much a blow at the wives and families of the warriors as if they had been struck by the Hun." A Midland engineering stoppage in July was ended only by threats to conscript the strikers. London bus and tram workers struck in August, as did Yorkshire miners. There were stoppages among cotton workers and railway men. Most surprising was a strike of London policemen in August. All these disputes reflected not only rising prices, but also sheer exhaustion and four years of increasing nervous stress.

Spanish Influenza

Following in the wake of war came the great influenza pandemic, said to have killed twenty-seven million people throughout the world in 1918 and 1919. No one knew where it began: some said in the festering slums of Bombay, others in the rat and lice infested trenches in France. The Press first noticed it in Spain: hence its popular name "Spanish influenza." The particularly virulent virus travelled swiftly with the armies and found easy victims in a half-starved Europe.

It arrived in Britain in June 1918. Three great waves of the disease killed 150,000 people across the country by May 1919, the worst epidemic since the cholera outbreak of the 1840's. Young adults were particularly affected, and death came suddenly from pneumonia. Undertakers were unable to cope. The tragedy of the war casualties was swollen by the huge civilian obituary columns. There was little to protect the individual. One doctor wrote, "The disease simply had its way. It came like a thief in the night and stole treasure." People wore masks over mouth and nose; streets, buses and trains were sprayed with disinfectant; schools, cinemas, music-halls and theatres closed. Some city councils advised people not to shave, not to borrow books, not to shake hands. More eccentric remedies appeared in the Press. *The Times* advised wealthier readers to "drink half a bottle of light wine or glass of port at dinner" or "to take a hot bath each evening." Snuff "slays the insidious bacillus with great effect." Nevertheless, three-quarters of the population were affected. The strange shadow of Spanish influenza was part of the exhaustion brought by the chaos of war. It was "the gleaner of war's harvest."

Spanish Influenza swept Europe in 1918, killing 150,000 in Britain by May 1919. This man is equipped to spray buses with disinfectant.

Armistice Day, 1918

The end of the war surprised everyone in Britain. The German advances spent themselves by July. Allied counterstrokes in the second Battle of the Marne pushed the enemy back. A massive British attack using four hundred tanks caused "the black day of the German Army," on 8th August when the whole front began to collapse. In September and October, Germany's allies, Bulgaria, Turkey and finally Austria surrendered. The German Generals, depressed by near revolution at home and mutiny in the navy, began negotiations for an Armistice. The many victories of the allied autumn advance had been greeted with scepticism by the British public. The headlines – "Great Allied Advance," "Allies

Right. Armistice Day 1918.
Patriotic girls celebrating.

Below. W.R.A.F.s delighted by
the end of the war.

Sweep forward," "The Flowing tide" – seemed merely the usual half truths. Even Lord Northcliffe (1865–1922), the Press Lord, said in September, "None of us will live to see the end of the war." Rumours of an approaching end mounted through October, although it was admitted that the German Army was still dangerous, like "a wounded man-eating tiger." The Diehards in the Press insisted on a decisive crushing victory. Horatio Bottomley demanded: "Destroy the Blond Beast." He continued: "Beware or the politicians will let the blond brutes of Middle Europe loose upon the world once more to procreate their lustful and bloody breed and pollute the human race with their lewd, coarse and savage strain . . . The people's mandate is – Destroy the Beast."

On 11th November, at 11 a.m. the Armistice brought the Great War to an end. In London the maroons were fired. Church bells across the country broke their long silence in an ecstacy of joyful ringing. Newspaper bills, long banished as a paper economy, suddenly re-appeared to announce, "Fighting has ceased on all fronts." As the hour struck, wrote Mrs. Peel, "It seemed almost as if one heard a dead silence and then that the whole nation gave a sigh of relief. A few moments later the people had gone mad." From his window at the Ministry of Munitions, Winston Churchill saw thousands of people streaming into the streets, shouting and screaming with joy. Showers of official forms were hurled from office windows to mark an end to wartime bureaucracy. Flags appeared as if by magic to brighten the grey November day. Buses and taxis were soon loaded, inside and out, with soldiers and civilians. Everyone gave up work for the day. Boy Scouts raced through the streets, sounding the final "All Clear" on their bugles. A deep roaring cheer rose from thousands of throats, supplemented by "The hooting of motors, the ringing of hand bells, the banging of tea trays, the shrilling of police whistles, and the screaming of toy trumpets." Hilarious crowds outside Buckingham Palace, in a strange echo of August 1914, called joyfully for the King. There was dancing in Trafalgar Square, and a bonfire, lit by Dominion soldiers on the plinth of Nelson's Column, scarred the monument permanently.

Amid this riotous joy that lasted three whole days, there were odd individual scenes. Top-hatted city men marched solemnly behind a band of kettles filled with rattling stones. Young officers carried a huge teddy bear, draped in Union Jacks. A crippled soldier waved a Belgian flag, and charwomen and wounded soldiers danced solemnly round a Scottish bagpiper. Dogs had red, white and blue ribbons tied to their tails. A group of medical students carried a skeleton marked "Hang the Kaiser." It was the dancers who seemed best able to express a joy that words could not. A man described to Mrs. Peel how he saw near Charing Cross "Two old women in prehistoric-looking bonnets and capes dancing stiffly and slowly to a barrel organ . . . played by a man so ancient that he looked as if he should have had a scythe rather than a hurdy gurdy."

As dusk fell, and despite the drizzle, bonfires and torch-lit processions lit up the night; street and shop lights again blazed boldly. In music halls, noted *The Times* reporter, "The air was full of the intoxicating spirit of joy. Audiences were a-quiver with half suppressed feeling and

The scene outside Buckingham Palace on Armistice Day.

ready to give it vent . . . It only needed half a dozen people to start a patriotic song – and the whole assembly would be on its feet and taking up the singing." Outside, searchlights swept crazily across the sky. The lights seemed to Macdonagh a symbol of the coming of peace: "Light! Light! Let there be Light! . . . For too long have we been under the shadow of Death and Destruction. Our faces are now set forward – looking towards the light of life."

Although relief was the first impact of the Armistice, the national mood was also tinged with sorrow. Throughout the country people queued outside churches and cathedrals to attend the many thanksgiving services, and to pray for the dead. "I sorrowed for the millions of young men who had lost their lives," wrote Macdonagh, "and perhaps more so for the wives whose reawakened spirit must in this hour of triumph be unbearably poignant". Soldiers, although glad that fear of death was lifted from them, grieved for dead comrades. To many, the victory seemed to have come too late: the soldier writer, Lord Dunsany, wrote a "Dirge to Victory."

> "Lift not thy trumpet, Victory, to the Sky
> Nor through battalions nor by batteries blow,
> But over hollows full of old wire go,
> Where, among dregs of war, the long dead lie
> With wasted iron that the guns passed by . . ."

In brighter mood, the popular song of the hour was full of hope for new life, now that the killing was done.

> "The bells are ringing
> For me and my girl
> The birds are singing
> For me and my girl . . ."

As the wild celebrations, which out-did even Mafeking day during the Boer War, subsided, everyday reality reasserted itself. Macdonagh felt some regret for the end of an era full of strange excitement: "A melancholy took possession of one when I came to realize . . . that a great and unique episode in my life was past and gone . . . Our sense of the value of life and its excitement so vividly heightened by the war, is, with one final leap of its flame today, about to expire in its ashes. Tomorrow we return to the monotonous and the humdrum . . ."

Opposite. Peace Day, celebrated in July 1919. From the *Illustrated London News*.

6 *Afterwards*

"Lovely word flying like a bird across the narrow seas,
When winter is over and songs are in the skies,
Peace . . ."

Laurence Binyon, *The Four Years*

745,000 BRITISH SOLDIERS DIED IN THE GREAT WAR. A further one and
and half million were seriously wounded. The loss of one in ten of
British men under 45 meant a definite shift in the population balance
between male and female, the bleak statistics concealing intense
personal suffering. The loss to the community was severe.

Every town and village proudly unveiled its local war memorial.
Most moving are the simplest, the wooden trench crosses, smeared with
Flanders mud, brought back from the front to be preserved in village
churches. In London, the Cenotaph in Whitehall was the national
memorial. Until the 1930's men used to raise their hats to it as they
passed. The Unknown Warrior, an anonymous corpse, was brought back
to Britain with great ceremonial to be buried in Westminster Abbey,
in remembrance of the thousands of men who had simply disappeared
in battle. The 11th November remained as the day of National Mourning, with the two minutes silence scrupulously observed at 11 a.m.
People stood still, and traffic stopped. A *Times* reporter described the
two minutes silence in 1919, as he stood at Buckingham Palace: "the
maroons sounded . . . and from a great babel of noise and confusion
arose the greater silence . . . the men uncovered. As I stood there . . .
'sorrow's keenest wind' cut across many memories. . . Names tumbled
over each other – young promising, keen lads – how many are now
filling lonely graves in France and Flanders? Everything was still.
Motor engines had stopped. Through the trees the streams of vehicles
to the north could be seen halted and people, people everywhere were
standing with bared heads – and handkerchiefs. This was the nation's
tribute to its great dead." Grieving relatives made melancholy Cook's
tours to visit the Western Front wastelands, where sons, fathers, brothers,
husbands had died. Certain British towns even linked themselves to
the tiny, shattered Flemish or French villages that their menfolk had
died defending or capturing.

Soon after the Armistice, Lloyd George called a General Election,
still standing himself as head of the coalition. His promises, which fitted
the public mood, won him a majority. Lloyd George took his "khaki
election" pledge to "Make Germany pay" to the 1919 Versailles Peace
Conference, which imposed harsh terms on the defeated enemy. However, another popular slogan, "Hang the Kaiser," was never fulfilled.
Instead the new idealism of the League of Nations tempered the bitter
feelings of revenge. This hope for a better world was reflected in the
Peace Day celebrations, held throughout Britain in July 1919.

Opposite. The Cenotaph in
London, the major memorial
to "the Glorious Dead."
From the *Illustrated London
News*.

Two minutes' silence:
a young widow grieves over
her husband's medal.

At home Lloyd George had another election promise to live up to.
"What is our task?" he had said in a famous speech... "To make Britain
a fit country for heroes to live in." Those who voted him to power
genuinely hoped for real social reform. The Education Act of 1918
seemed promising; it was followed by the Housing and Town Planning
Act of 1919, proposing large scale building of local authority "Council
houses" of good quality to make amends for the shortage of 600,000
dwellings caused by war. The Unemployment Insurance Act of 1920
was a third major benefit, giving payment to those out of work, while
the Ministry of Health Act of 1919 promised more medical care for
ordinary people. In 1920 the future, therefore, seemed full of promise.
The streets were again brightly lit, and returning soldiers found work
easily.

By 1921, the wartime industrial boom was finished. Industrialists
were finding that British markets in the world had disappeared. There
were now too many ships on the seas to make ship building profitable.
Oil was already superseding coal as a fuel, especially in ships. The great
British primary industries therefore began to suffer. The huge war
debts began to be felt. Unemployment rose rapidly to two million by
mid-1921. Wages fell, and cuts were announced, under the Government's "Geddes Axe," in public expenditure. The hopeful Housing and
Education reforms were first to suffer. "Homes fit for heroes" began to

sound a hollow promise. So began the long inter-war slump, in which unemployment never fell below a million. The returned soldiers suffered a final disillusion. For many, an escape from the trench world of "mud and stench and underground gloom" led only to the grey life of unemployment or soul-destroying, inadequate work. George Coppard described the post-war world in his autobiography, *With a Machine Gun to Cambrai*: "Although an expert machine-gunner, I was a numbskull so far as any trade or craft was concerned . . . and I joined the queues for jobs as messengers, window cleaners and scullions. It was a complete let-down for thousands like me, and for some young officers too. It was a common sight in London to see ex-officers with barrel-organs, endeavouring to earn a living as beggars. . ."

By the mid 1920s reaction against the very memory of the war had set in among old soldiers, who now looked back bitterly on Armistice Day. The poet Sherard Vines provided such a judgement on the war, in his "War Commemoration 1925:"

A dismal peace: a former soldier tries to earn a living.

> "We must remember the weary stand-to
> Of millions, pale in corpse-infected mist,
> The mad, and those turned monsters . . .
>
> . . . And how, unseen,
> Dark Mania sat in offices, and designed
> New schemes for shambles, learning year by year
> Painfully, secretly, to degrade the world."

Table of Dates

1914 *June* 28 Archduke Franz Ferdinand assassinated at Sarajevo.
June 30 London Stock Exchange closed.
Aug. 4 Germans entered Belgium after declaring war on France (Aug. 3). Great Britain declared war on Germany.
Aug. 6 Kitchener's first appeal for 100,000 volunteers for the New Armies.
Aug 7 Defence of The Realm Act passed in principle (D.O.R.A.).
Aug. 9 British Expeditionary Force landed in France.
Spymania in Britain.
Aug. 25 Retreat from Mons began.
Sept. 11 Blackout in London.
Dec. 16 German naval attack on Yorkshire coast.
Dec. 24 First German air-raid on Dover.

1915 *Jan.* 19 First Zeppelin raid on Norfolk
March 10 Battle of Neuve Chapelle.
April 25 Gallipoli Landings.
May 7 Sinking of the *Lusitania*.
Anti-German riots in Britain.
May 21 The shell shortage scandal.
May 25 Asquith formed Coalition Government.
June 16 Lloyd George made Minister of Munitions.
July 17 Women's "Right to Serve" rally in London.
Aug. 15 National Register; The Derby Scheme.
Sept. 8 Zeppelin raid on London.
Sept. 25 Battle of Loos.

1916 *Jan.* 8 First Military Service Act introduced Conscription.
Tribunals set up to hear Conscientious Objectors.
May 21 Introduction of Summer Time to aid war work.
May 31 Battle of Jutland.
July 1 Battle of the Somme began: Kitchener's Armies in action.
Sept. 2 Zeppelin shot down at Cuffley.
Dec. 6 Lloyd George became Prime Minister.

1917 *Jan.* 29 Silvertown Arsenal explosion.
Feb. 1 Unrestricted submarine war declared by Germany.
April 6 U.S.A. declared war on Germany.
June 13 Gotha raid on London.
July 26 Lord Rhonnda appointed Food Controller.
July 31 Battle of Passchendaele.
Sept. Severe air-raids on London.

1918 *Jan.* Food queues in Britain.
Feb. 25 Rationing in London
Mar. 21 German Western Front offensive began.
June "Votes for Women" passed in Parliament.
Aug. 8 British Victory at Amiens "The Black Day of the German Army."
Oct. Spanish influenza epidemic.
Nov. 11 Armistice concluded.

Further Reading

General Works

The Deluge, Arthur Marwick (Bodley Head, 1965; Pelican).
English History 1914–1945, A. J. P. Taylor (Oxford, 1965; Pelican).
The Home Fronts: Britain, France, Germany 1914–18, John Williams (Constable, 1972).
The Great War, ed. H. W. Wilson and J. A. Hammerton, 13 vols (Amalgamated Press, 1914–19). (Various articles, especially those by Harold Owen.)
How we lived then 1914–18, C. S. Peel (Bodley Head, 1929).
Society at War 1914–16, Caroline Playne (Allen & Unwin, 1931).
Britain Holds On 1917–18, Caroline Playne (Allen & Unwin, 1933).
The Home Front, Sylvia Pankhurst (Hutchinson, 1932).
In London During The Great War, Michael Macdonagh (Eyre & Spottiswoode, 1935).

Particular Topics

AIR RAIDS
The Zeppelin in Combat, D. Robinson (Foulis, 1962).
The First Battle of Britain, N. Fredette (Cassell, 1965).
WOMEN'S WORK
Women on the Warpath, D. Mitchell (Cape, 1966).
CONSCIENTIOUS OBJECTORS
Objection Overruled, D. Boulton (MacGibbon & Kee, 1967).
PROPAGANDA
Posters of the First World War, M. Richards (Adams & Dart, 1968).

Literary accounts

Testament of Youth, Vera Brittain (Gollancz, 1933; Grey Arrow). (Moving experiences of a V.A.D. Nurse.)
Goodbye to All That, Robert Graves (Penguin).
Memoirs of George Sherston (*Fox Hunting Man, Infantry Officer, Sherston's Progress*), Siegfried Sassoon (Faber).
Mr. Britling Sees it through, H. G. Wells (Cassell, 1916; Corgi). (Life in England up to 1916.)
Kangaroo D. H. Lawrence (Penguin). (The chapter "The Nightmare"

describes moods and experiences in wartime.)
Collected Letters of D. H. Lawrence, ed. H. T. Moore (Heinemann, 1965).
Short Stories of D. H. Lawrence, especially "Tickets Please" and "Monkey Nuts" concerned with women's work in War. (Penguin).
"Mary Postgate" in *The Friendly Brook and other stories*, Rudyard Kipling (Penguin). (A study of wartime hate.)
Sagittarius Rising, Cecil Lewis (Peter Davies 1916; Corgi). (An R.F.C. pilot in Gotha raids on London 1917.)

Poetry

Up the Line to Death: The War Poets 1914–18, B. Gardner (Methuen, 1964).
Collected Poems of Wilfred Owen, ed. C. Day Lewis (Chatto & Windus, 1967).
Selected Poems, Siegfried Sassoon (Faber, 1968).

Index

Acknowledgements

The publishers and author thank the following for loaning pictures used to illustrate this book: Radio Times Hulton Picture Library, pp. 8 (left), 11 (top), 22–3, 25, 32, 41, 70 (top), 71, 73 (bottom), 83 (bottom), 87, 104 (bottom), 108 (right), 111 (bottom), 115–6; Trustees of the Imperial War Museum, jacket picture, pp. 17 (right), 21, 29–30, 33, 45–7, 49, 58–62, 63 (top), 65, 66 (top), 75, 82, 86, 90–1, 102, 103 (bottom), 111 (top), 114 (top); Trustees of the British Museum, p. 18 (top); Mansell Collection, pp. 18 (bottom), 27–8, 31, 37, 48, 66 (bottom), 67 (top), 69 (top), 72 (bottom), 73 (top), 74 (bottom), 78, 95, 110, 112–13; The Peace Pledge Union, p. 54; Harold Bing, pp. 55–7; Barnaby's Picture Library, pp. 84, 122; Kodak Museum, pp. 96, 123.